Renew by phone or online

KT-194-371

www.____

Bristol Libraries

____ STAMPED

They Started It!

Bristol Library Service

AN 3113148 4

PRENTICE HALL LIFE

If life is what you make it, then making it better starts here.

What we learn today can change our lives tomorrow. It can change our goals or change our minds; open up new opportunities or simply inspire us to make a difference. That's why we have created a new breed of books that do more to help you make more of your life.

Whether you want more confidence or less stress, a new skill or a different perspective, we've designed *Prentice Hall Life* books to help you make a change for the better. Together with our authors, we share a commitment to bring you the brightest ideas and best ways to manage your life, work and wealth.

In these pages we hope you'll find the ideas you need for the life you want.

Go on, help yourself.

It's what you make it.

They started it!

How to help your kids get along better

Sacha Baveystock

BRISTOL CITY COUNCIL	
Askews	11-Dec-2007
649.143	£9.99

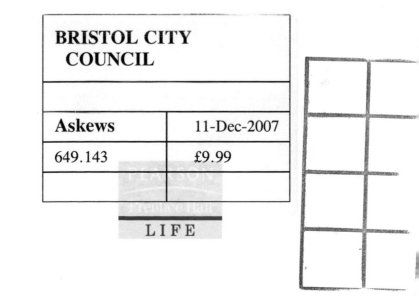

PEARSON

Prentice Hall

LIFE

Pearson Education Limited
Edinburgh Gate
Harlow
Essex CM20 2JE
England

© Sacha Baveystock 2007

First published 2007

The right of Sacha Baveystock to be identified as author of this Work
has been asserted by her in accordance with the Copyright, Designs and
Patents Act, 1988.

All rights reserved. No part of this publication may be reproduced,
stored in a retrieval system or transmitted in any form or by any means
electronic, mechanical, photocopying, recording, or otherwise, without
either the prior written permission of the publishers and copyright
owners or a licence permitting restricted copying in the United Kingdom
issued by the Copyright Licensing Agency Ltd, 90 Tottenham Court Road,
London W1T 4LP.

ISBN 978-0-273-71264-0

Commissioning editor: Emma Shackleton
Project editor: Belinda Wilkinson
Designer: Kevin O'Connor
Cover designer: Annette Peppis
Cover illustration: Chris Long
Senior production controller: Man Fai Lau

Printed and bound by Henry Ling, UK
The Publisher's policy is to use paper manufactured from sustainable
forests.

Contents

CONTENTS

Introduction

One summer day, whilst pregnant with my third child, I took my elder children to an adventure park. I was sitting on a bench in a crowded area when suddenly two children started screeching at each other. Within seconds they had graduated to spitting, jostling and grabbing at each other's hair, while their parents screamed at them: 'Stop it! That's enough!'

'Right, that's it!' yelled the mother, as the boy propelled his sister to the ground. 'I'm not spending another minute with you two. I can't bring you anywhere!' She walked off, leaving the children with their father, who shrieked after her that *he* couldn't cope with them. 'Now look what you've done!' he told them. 'Your fighting has ruined our day out.' At that moment the mother reappeared, still raging, and declared they were all going home. Everyone watched with open mouths as she hauled her now sobbing children and glowering husband off towards the car park.

A small crowd of onlookers exchanged knowing glances and assumed 'holier than thou' expressions. How embarrassing. A family day out in tatters; tempers out of control, the children ruining time that should have been for them. I sat there rather smugly pitying the parents. Thank goodness I didn't have children like that.

Wind the clock forward four years and I'm sitting on a lovely beach. We're on holiday, the sun is shining and all should be well – only the baby I was carrying four years previously has just viciously and wilfully destroyed the sand castle that his older brother has been carefully moulding for the past hour. His older brother has punched him to the ground and the four-year-old is now on his brother's back tearing at his cheek. Both are screaming and crying, while their older sister is yelling and goading them, fuelling the flames. I can feel the eyes of half the beach upon me, waiting for me to intervene. I, too, have an overwhelming desire to walk off and leave them all behind…Why, oh *why* do they have to fight like this?

Did I do something wrong? Is this a normal healthy part of kids' growing up or a sign of a family in trouble? And what do I do now?

Why I'm writing this book

As one of four children and a mother of three, I know a bit about fighting siblings. A few years ago I started making the parenting TV series *Little Angels* and *Teen Angels* for the BBC. I had just returned to work after having my third child, and it seemed a perfect dovetailing of life and work. By day I worked with a team of psychologists, putting together programmes about families who were having problems with their children's behaviour, and then when I went home I got to put the theory into practice. I learnt an enormous amount about how to encourage and motivate good behaviour, and how to deal with the behaviour I didn't want. The broad message of the series was that if you put boundaries in place and found clear ways of communicating with your children, then your chances of enjoying family life would be all the greater.

It sounds rather glib, but there's no doubt that the way you perceive your children and interact with them has a profound influence both on how they behave and how they in turn treat others. While making the programmes, it was striking to witness how a few simple changes on the part of the parents could indeed make all the difference to how their kids behaved.

But it was also clear, in making the programmes, that family dynamics can be extremely complicated and none more so than the relationship between siblings. I came across many families where tensions and differences between siblings of varying ages were making life hell for their family, and there wasn't always a quick fix for children who didn't get on. I was curious to find out more.

Meanwhile, despite all that practice making parenting programmes, my own children, now aged nine, seven and four, seemed to live in a perpetual state of friction, veering between petty bickering to all-out war on a daily basis. I know (or think I know) that deep down they love each other, but the constant competitiveness and conflict were wearing me down.

So I decided to find out more about the causes of sibling rivalry and how we, as parents, can make a difference to the way siblings interact. Is conflict inevitable, or can it be prevented? Why is it so much worse in some families than in others? Which bits can parents make a difference with and which not? To get to the heart of what can make or break this most complicated of relationships, I talked to psychologists, child behaviour experts, sibling researchers and, of course, lots of parents.

When I told one mother I was writing this book, she smiled and said, 'Maybe you can discover *the* secret for stopping children fighting and then you can patent it and sell it worldwide!' Fantasy indeed, but I hope it is possible to tease out at least some of the reasons why children fight, and what – if anything – you can do about it. And since my own children are so busy providing me with material, they've helped me put a few techniques to the test in my bid to bring peace to our family home.

A *unique relationship*

Of course, siblings don't just fight. There's no doubt that being a sibling is one of the most intense and extraordinary relationships any of us can have. 'Their experiences are part of your life's adventure,' observed one mother of her own siblings, and this is certainly true for me. When, for example, I went to stay with my brother, who was living in Australia, I ended up meeting my husband there.

So long as accident or illness don't intervene, your siblings are going to be one of the most constant presences throughout your entire life. Yet for some people, the rivalry and dislike they experience as children can last a lifetime too. I know of several people who no longer speak to their siblings. Some have fallen out over adult grievances, like inheritance disputes, or a dislike of each other's partners, but for many the rivalry stretches right back through the years to early childhood.

'The relationship is about so much more than rivalry,' observes Professor Judy Dunn, who has spent much of her career tracking how sibling relationships develop.

All the stuff we've learned from observing siblings has been important in changing our understanding of child development. It's a relationship where you learn so much about other people, and develop

4

key skills in knowing both how to irritate and to comfort. A sibling knows very well what upsets another child and that can work for good or evil. Even by the age of two, a sibling can make the connection between what another child finds upsetting – and then doing it.

Most experts agree that much of the squabbling that goes on between siblings is a natural and invaluable way of acquiring life skills, such as tolerance and give and take. It also teaches us the limits of one's patience and strength. If I had not had siblings, who else in my life would have hidden under my bed, pretending to be a werewolf; switched off the light from the outside, when I was in the bath; forced a whole pair of socks into my mouth; perfected a technique of hitting me with a flip flop (known as the Flip Flop Flack); and repeatedly chanted my disliked second name until I was on the brink of committing murder? Who would have joined me in secret clubs, in making up languages (which drove our parents mad) and in playing numerous pranks – from sampling tumblers of our parents' crème de menthe, to throwing ripe peaches through neighbours' open windows? Many of the occasions in my life, when I've laughed until I cried, have been with my siblings. As teenagers, my brothers and I shared friends, music and a few hairy adventures. My sister – who told me recently that she used to hate me – is today a good friend, whom I see as often as living in different cities allows. Life with siblings can be tremendous fun, and in families such as mine, where children outnumber adults, it can be a great recipe for mischief-making and anarchy. A sibling can be an accomplice, a confidante, protector and friend.

Successful sibling relationships can also help lay the foundations for other relationships, by teaching us how to appreciate someone else's point of view. Siblings are constantly watching and learning from each other, using the competition between them to build up skills they can apply in their dealings with others. That's the plus side. The down side is that learning about someone else's point of view isn't always a genteel business. And as a parent, that can be hard to watch.

Can parents make a difference?

'You know the best way of preventing sibling rivalry?' father of four, Ian, asked me. 'Don't have more than one child'. I take his point (he clearly didn't). But is that the limit of what parents can do in ensuring whether their children get on?

Some parents seem to maintain a slightly superior position on how wonderfully their children get along. Sometimes, when I tell people my children fight relentlessly, they look at me politely and say, 'Really?' One posting I made on a parenting website got a very pointed reply: 'My children respect each other.'

But I know that I'm far from alone. A poll of my friends and colleagues on their own sibling relationships yielded the following memories:

I put a large crab with its claw near my sister's ear so it bit her and hung on. It had to be killed to get it off.

My sister used to throw shoes at me when we shared a room, and I don't mean playfully. Normally she aimed at the face.

INTRODUCTION

My brothers often subjected me to the Nuremberg trials: tied to a chair and questioned for hours. Missed lunch.

I was so jealous of my sister's abundantly dark curly hair I cut it all off. When it grew back, it was straight.

I spat in the bread I was baking. I enjoyed watching my brother eat his sandwich all the more.

Clearly this is a relationship like no other. With such extremes of light and shade, knowing when to get involved and when to let children get on with being, well, children can be a tough call for parents.

Certainly my poll also revealed that many siblings ride out huge storms during childhood only to find friendship as adults:

I hated my sister while we were living at home, but now we see each other every day.

My brother teased me relentlessly when we were little. Now he's my rock, there for me in a way that no one else is.

But it's also apparent that some siblings never really find common ground:

My brother and I still talk but if we weren't related, I doubt we'd be more than acquaintances.

*I'll never stop resenting my sister. I still get a knot
in my stomach when she phones.*

The temptation might be to just stand back and let what
will be be. Certainly Lisa, a mother of five, thinks so. 'The
secret to having happy and loving siblings is quite simply
this,' she says. 'Struggle through their formative years,
aided by whichever method works for your family, good old-
fashioned bribery, whatever, and guaranteed, when they are
grown up, they'll all be meeting down the pub anyway.'

But educational psychologist Laverne Antrobus sees
the job of helping siblings get on as 'a huge task'. 'Parents
can have a rather rosy picture of how they think their
children will get along and often the reality is very different,'
she reflects.

*These expectations are important but can be
unreasonable. Learning to live together is complex,
children have very different personalities and these
need to be accommodated into a family system.
The approach that you take as a parent is key, if
you are trying to mould and push your children
into positions that they do not want to take up then
tensions will arise.*

Psychotherapist Julie Lynn-Evans, who works with many
children with emotional and behavioural problems,
estimates that up to a third of the children she sees have
issues with sibling rivalry. She thinks it is important to
make a very clear distinction between what can be seen as
the usual jockeying for position and boundary-testing that
goes on between children, and more sinister, deliberate

unpleasantness. 'Parents shouldn't be afraid of sibling rivalry,' she suggests. 'Competition is great for honing skills like negotiating and compromise, for learning what you will and won't take. But when the behaviour becomes toxic and premeditated, or is harmful, that's when parents need to do something about it.'

So, while it would be unrealistic to hope to get rid of sibling rivalry, how we handle it may have a continuing impact on our children's lives. How children get on with each other can affect their entire view of relationships throughout their lives; if we can help siblings get off to a good start together, they may be better equipped to weather the inevitable squalls of adult relationships.

Just as importantly, we have to live with our children while they are growing up and, if the house is a war zone, it's unpleasant for everyone. It stands to reason that the less screeching and bloodletting there is, the less stressful it is going to be for us as parents. It is worth fostering cooperative sibling relationships to ensure that there's a bit of peace in the house, which is why I had to get to work because, in my household at least, this is how it was going:

A day in a life...

Breakfast time

Mother is making breakfast.
Daughter (D) comes in and greets younger son (YS).

YS: Go away!

D: No, this is my house too, so shut up! Baby! Toddler!

YS: I'm not a toddler. [*Sits in the middle of the floor and lashes out as she walks past.*]

D: Ow! Shut up you podgy baby.

YS: [*Screams.*] I'm not podgy. [*Whacks her again.*]

Mother manages to get children to table, and calm is briefly restored.

D: Stop taking all the honey! [*Snatches the container out of his hand.*]

YS: [*Piercing shriek.*]

D: We share in this family. So shut up! [*She pointedly tweaks him as she moves past.*]

YS: Mum, she's being really mean to me today.

D: Yes I am, because you're a baby. Mum! He just wiped butter on my dress – why aren't you telling him off?

Later, while getting ready for school
D to elder son (ES): Smarty-pants, homework-loving boy who doesn't like sports. Hee, hee, hee!

ES: Shut up! Just shut up, stop it!' [*Loud piercing scream.*]

D: I'm not doing anything; I'm brushing my hair.

ES: Yes you are, you're being annoying.

D: Hello girly.

ES: Fat butthead! [*Whips her with the pyjama top he's holding.*] Shutuuuuuuuuuuuppppp!

D: What a baby.

So where do I begin? At the beginning of course...

CHAPTER ONE

We don't need another baby

It's a familiar conversation. 'And how does little Jim like his new sister?' you ask the glowing mother who has just produced her second child. 'Oh,' beams the mother. 'He absolutely *adores* her!' 'What makes you so sure?' you want to ask, but it would be unkind. We all want our children to get along, and it is at this crucial turning point, when one becomes two, that sibling rivalry is primed to begin. Parents worry that, if they get this bit wrong, their children will be at daggers drawn forevermore.

I'll never forget the expression on my daughter's face as she stood in the doorway of the hospital room where I lay with her new brother beside me on the bed. Her eyes took on a hooded quality I hadn't seen before; hesitation, suspicion and what looked like dismay all flickered across her two-year-old face. Later when we were home from the hospital, I saw the same look again. Her father was dancing in the kitchen with the baby in his arms, something he had done with her, as a baby, too. Again her eyes became hooded and suspicious. Clearly from her point of view this wasn't quite the cracking idea we'd made out it was going to be. Sometimes I wonder if she has ever forgiven her brother for that moment.

It seems likely that the first-born who has been knocked off his pedestal and lost the singular attention of his parents forever is going to be the most obvious candidate for later sibling resentment, and the caseload of psychotherapist Julie Lynn-Evans suggests that there is some truth in this. A large proportion of the children with sibling issues she sees are infuriated older siblings who have never got over the appearance of their brother or sister. 'What I see a lot of is where the elder ones still don't believe the younger siblings have got a right to their place in the world and are still furious that they were born,' she says. 'They want them to be sent anywhere but the home in which they live. They would be happy if their younger siblings ceased to exist.'

Clearly these resentments have taken some years to build; by the time these particular children reach the therapist's office they are often aged between seven and ten. But if parents want to prevent their children ending up in therapy, can the seeds of a good relationship – if not adoration – be sown from the very beginning?

Getting off to a good start

The reassuring news (or troubling, depending on how you look at it) is that at least 50 per cent of children – and in some studies this goes as high as 90 per cent – show some level of behavioural problems after the birth of a sibling, including hostility, aggression and disturbed behaviour.

If your child screams, shouts, reverts to more childish behaviour and even takes a swing at the baby, you're certainly not alone. But you can take some comfort from the evidence from long-term sibling studies: that reaction, however extreme it is, doesn't necessarily indicate that the relationship is going to be troubled for life. And while there is much you *can* do as a parent to ensure that siblings get off to a good start together, the way your child reacts isn't entirely down to you.

Professor Judy Dunn, who has conducted several long-term studies into sibling relationships thinks it's important for parents to recognize this. 'It wouldn't be justified to suggest that the expression of jealousy and disturbance depends entirely on the parents,' she insists. 'You can't underestimate the part played by temperament.'

Children show marked differences from the very beginning and whether a child is laid-back and easy-going, or moody and intense in the way he reacts to things, can make a huge difference to how he will adapt to the birth of a sibling. A child who is volatile, who gets upset at changes in routine, or new experiences, such as meeting strangers, is likely to react more intensely than an easy-going child. A more placid or amenable character, who is better able to go with the flow, is likely to have fewer problems dealing with the upheaval that a new baby brings; and the temperament of the baby can have an impact, too. If he is fussy or colicky, then he might be harder to manage, which could also affect the sibling relationship.

So, taking comfort from the fact that not all children are tailor-made to fit together, what can you do to try and ensure that the transition is as smooth as possible?

Easing the blow

Undoubtedly life after the birth of a sibling can be hugely
unsettling for any child. But while you've had a baby before
and know that things are going to adapt and settle, this is a
completely alien experience for a first-born. The world as he
knows it is going to change forever – in a positive way, of
course – but it's not surprising if this causes uncertainty and
distress.

When to tell your child about her impending sibling
is the first thing to think about. 'I remember when I had my
second child, the doctor told me not to bother my two-year-
old son by talking about the baby before the event as he
wouldn't understand,' recalls Pauline, who had her children
in the 1950s and is now a grandmother. 'He reacted terribly
badly when I brought the baby home.' These days few of
us would think of springing a ready-made sibling on our
unsuspecting first-born, but it is possible to swing too far in
the other direction.

Although it helps a child to have plenty of advance
warning, it doesn't help to tell a very young child too early.
He can't really conceptualize something in the distant future
and, if you tell him before there is even a visible bump,
it will be too far off for him to take on board. Even a few
weeks is an eternity in the life of a small child and he might
get bored with all this talk about a baby who then doesn't
arrive. Dates that are pegged to other events of which he is
aware might help: 'after our summer holiday', for instance,
or 'before your birthday' might give some sense of time.

What does help is to involve the elder child in the
preparations, so that she simply becomes used to the idea
that something is happening. When I was pregnant with
my third child, I took my elder son along with me on many

of the antenatal visits, mostly through necessity rather than choice. He was fascinated by seeing his younger brother on ultrasound, and loved the sound of the baby's heartbeat through the Doppler machine, which he liked to describe as 'galloping horses'. Of course, if the pregnancy is problematic in any way, this might not be practical.

Extra tips to prepare your child for another baby

Point out and spend time with babies wherever you can. It's important for elder children to realize that a new baby initially isn't going to be a 'playmate', but a helpless creature who won't do much for a while, except sleep and eat. Be realistic about the fact that the baby might not be much fun.

It helps to emphasize the older child's 'bigness': not only how she will be able to help Mum and Dad with the baby, but all the fun things the poor little baby won't be able to do, like eating cake, going to playgroup or riding bikes.

Show your child baby pictures of herself and talk about what her needs were as a baby: how she fed from breast or bottle and needed winding.

Use toys to act out what you do with babies. We used my daughter's bear to practise endless nappy changing and how to comfort crying, while my elder son took a doll he called his baby to bed with him for some months.

Read lots of books. Our favourite was *Za Za's Baby Brother*, which describes well the big sister's feelings of being left out by the new baby demanding so much attention, and points out that Mum and Dad are extremely busy and tired after the baby first comes.

If you're going to need to move your child out of his cot or room to make way for the new baby, do it in plenty of time. If he's moving room, put a positive spin on it and let him 'give' his room to the baby, help you choose colours and generally seem in charge. If the child is going to experience other changes, such as a new carer, or more time with his grandparents when the baby comes, it's worth setting these things up in advance too.

Encourage your older child's friendships with other children. One study found that having a close playmate helps children interact with their younger brothers and sisters, perhaps because it teaches them some of the social skills they need.

When the baby arrives, there is that all-important first visit. It helps not to be holding or feeding the baby when an older sibling comes to the hospital, and don't expect her to make a big fuss of the baby. Instead make a big fuss of *her* for being so clever. Psychologist Laverne Antrobus says:

> *Often a situation as simple as who the grandparents fuss over can make a child feel very let down and left out. A cute baby will attract all the attention, so ask visitors to pay attention to your other child before rushing to the baby. This will speak volumes to your child about where he comes in the pecking order.*

Some people like to have a present ready for the older child from the baby. Children love the idea that the baby brought something just for them. My daughter still remembers the toy kitten in a carry box, which came with her youngest brother; for a long time she thought it had been tucked into my belly alongside him.

Despite my preparation, my daughter wasn't exactly jumping for joy when her first brother arrived, and I don't know whether I could have done much more to encourage adoration. But three years later, when her second brother was born, she was skipping down the hospital corridor determined to be first to hold the baby. It took her time to adapt but she embraced the role of older sister.

Why should little Jim adore his baby sister from the word go? In truth, a new baby is a huge change, and it would be unrealistic to expect a first-born child not to feel it. Advance warning won't necessarily prevent negative feelings, but to recognize that those feelings are there, rather than deny them, will help a lot.

Playing up

When you are completely absorbed with all the needs and delights of a new baby, it's hard for a child to appreciate that the focus of your world has shifted. Meanwhile it can be equally hard for you as a parent to remember that you are still at the centre of *his* world, only suddenly a whole lot less available.

It's hardly surprising, as well as being very common, that elder siblings display a range of reactions: clinginess and anxiety, refusal to do things, anger or aggression. But, even if you're not surprised, it can be a struggle not to respond with impatience. Suddenly your first baby looks enormous and because the new baby is so much more needy, it's possible to slip into expecting far more of the older child than is realistic. It's important to make sure that your expectations of the elder child haven't suddenly shifted, so you're now intolerant of behaviour that simply reflects his age.

There's also another side to this behaviour: an elder child who is put out by the presence of the baby is going to quickly learn that the best way to get attention in a busy family is by playing up. What better way of getting attention than by having a tantrum, even if that attention is in the form of a telling off?

Experts recommend that one of the most important things you can do during the early weeks is to try to minimize changes to the elder child's life and, in particular, to avoid dropping the level of play and attention he gets from you. In the early weeks it's probably as much as you can do to factor in a bit of story or playtime in rare moments when the baby is asleep (and you're not). Having some extra privileges, such as staying up later when the baby has gone to bed, or special time, which the baby can't share, will appeal to an older child.

Many mothers describe how their older child will start to play up the moment they start to feed the baby, either running around or trying to crawl onto his mother's lap. 'The moment I sat down and got the baby latched on was the moment that he would start being whiney and difficult,' remembers Neela of her two-and-a-half-year-old Rohan. 'He would always suddenly need a drink, or a wee, or a toy that wasn't in the room – anything to distract me from the baby. Or he would disappear, so I had to go and see what he was up to; then the baby would start to scream for his feed.'

WE DON'T NEED ANOTHER BABY

Most children are going to display some worse than usual behaviour, and it's worth being prepared for ingenious boundary-testing. Professor Judy Dunn spent months visiting the homes of families with new siblings, observing the interactions between mothers and first-borns. She found that the frequency of children being 'deliberately naughty' increased threefold after the new baby arrived, mostly when the mother was busy with the baby. 'One little boy waited until his mother was feeding the baby and then went and let down the washing line into the mud, with all the clothes on it,' she recalls. 'Another sprinkled his milk all over the sofa, while pointedly looking at his mother who was completely absorbed with the baby.'

But what's heartening is that Dunn's findings suggest that even the most extreme reaction in a first-born does not mean a lifetime of conflict. 'A child who becomes demanding or difficult is not especially likely to get on badly with his brother or sister in later years,' she concluded. 'Just because they play up now doesn't mean it's all going to be awful.' Interestingly she found that it was the children who *didn't* react who remained more hostile to their sibling later on, particularly those who would withdraw into a world of their own.

'What we found from our study was that if the children had a comfort object or sucked their thumb, they would go into almost a trance-like state,' she says. 'For the mothers that may be very helpful, they're quiet and preoccupied. But they're the children who perhaps come out worst. The ones who were naughty had a better outcome.'

Finding ways to occupy your child while you are busy with the baby is key. 'The best advice I got was from a midwife who suggested that I get Rohan to help me make a goodie box full of special things he liked, which he could play with while I was feeding,' recalls Neela.

> *It worked really well. We kept adding to it, and he would show me stuff and chat with me more during the feed. Then as the baby got bigger I began to align his feeds more with Rohan's mealtimes. So long as he had my attention still, he didn't mind about the baby.*
>
> *She also told me not to train him to act up more by offering rewards, such as biscuits or sweets. I thought that was a really useful point. I know that if I'd started fobbing him off with biscuits, he would have kept right on pushing those buttons.*

Who's the baby?

With the baby getting all that lovely cuddling and attention, the eldest child might feel that there aren't many benefits to being the big one and that it's a better deal to be the baby. Regressive behaviour, such as bed-wetting, dummy or thumb sucking, or tantrums are all very common. It's not unusual to hear of children reverting to waking in the night, wanting a bottle again, or even lying in the baby gym.

But clinical psychologist Dr Stephen Briers thinks it's important for parents to understand what motivates the behaviour, and not to get too exercised by it. 'Toddlers get jealous because the baby is poaching the parent *and* their territory of being the younger child,' he says. 'It helps if you can accept it. Make time for your child to regress a little.'

Some children who have previously been dressing

themselves start asking for help again, or those who have been potty-trained suddenly revert to having accidents, or even needing to go back into nappies. Mostly it seems best to leave this to pass in its own time. I had been trying to potty-train my daughter before her brother was born but once he came along I realized that I had to let it go for a while. Eventually her desire to be a big girl while the baby was the one who wore the nappies helped her to make progress, but it took time.

The hardest regression to bear can be when a child, who was previously sleeping through the night, starts waking or getting up in the night. This needs the minimum of attention to discourage the child from getting into a pattern. Patricia's three-year-old son Andrew woke up to seven times a night for the first six months after his younger sister was born. 'It was a nightmare,' recalls Patricia, 'far more exhausting than the baby. It only stopped after we stopped giving him any attention when he called out for us. He needed to see that there was nothing to gain from getting up in the night.'

The baby's going to get it...

Everyone has an anecdote about the things jealous siblings have done to the hapless baby: the baby in the washing machine, in the vegetable drawer of the fridge, even drawing pins in the baby's cot. A health professional told one friend of mine that she should assume that every older sibling would in fact like their newborn sibling dead, and to take precautions accordingly.

There are some children who do seem hell-bent on hurting their sibling. When Trish gave birth to her second son, Tom, her first-born, eighteen-month-old Alex, did his best to cause trouble. 'He was a very intelligent eighteen-month-old, and it seemed that he decided that the best way to go about it was to remove Tom,' recalls Trish. 'He took a darning needle from the desk drawer and stuck it in his brother's head when he was just a month old.'

Luckily baby Tom was only superficially injured by the needle but more was to follow. Next Alex took a cushion and held it over the baby's head. And soon after that he bit his brother's finger. 'Tom didn't walk for a long time because Alex would push him over,' remembers Trish. 'I had to watch him all the time.' One day when Tom had started crawling, Trish was briefly distracted. Alex opened the front door and the baby crawled out onto the street. 'The first I knew of it was when I heard the screech of tyres and shouting in the street,' says Trish. Baby Tom was fine, but the pattern was set for years of rivalry.

For Lesley, now in her forties, her brother's attempts to 'kill' her as a newborn have become family folklore:

> *My mother tells me that when he was introduced to me he snatched the baby blanket off my cot and yelled: 'That's mine!' Later he threw a metal toy at me, which hit me on my head and cut it. After that I was kept in a locked room and only came out to be bathed and fed when he wasn't about. Still I like him well enough now.*

While such stories make great anecdotes, it wouldn't be fair or healthy to regard your child as a budding murderer. In truth there are probably a host of forces at work when a child does something to hurt his baby sibling: irritation, jealousy, a sense of curiosity, and a complete inability to know his own strength. Often these feelings slide into each other, and a young child who is feeling hacked off with the new set-up and wants to grab his parents' attention will quickly learn that having a go at the baby works a treat. Either way, babies should not be left alone with children under four who might be boisterous, aggressive or over inquisitive, and potential aggression will need firm and careful handling.

Sometimes a toddler is simply being overzealous and can crowd a baby sibling without any sense of her fragility. 'He thinks he's tickling his baby sister under the chin when he's practically strangling her,' says Tessa about her three-year-old son, Kai. The best response is to be clear and firm, but not to go overboard or label the child mean or naughty. You can also gently show a child the level of touch a baby needs without seeming critical of him. But, if you overreact, it might make him more determined to attack.

My newborn son was less than a week old when his two-year-old sister picked up a piece of cheese from the tea table and posted it into his mouth. I read this as curiosity rather than malice, but when she starting trying to body slam him as he lay on his mat, I was less certain. One afternoon she picked up his legs and pushed him across the wooden floor like a Hoover. I took care not to leave her alone with him, not because I thought she meant him any real harm but because she was unpredictable.

Recently I watched a scene on a family video of him being changed. She picks up his feet and begins to peddle them, then starts trying to fold him up in the changing mat. She stops when asked to, but later when I am holding the baby, she picks the whole mat up and tries to swamp both of us. Perhaps she did feel like smothering the pair of us.

Patiently explaining to the toddler, for the fifteenth time that day, why he shouldn't prod the baby can take its toll. 'Kai is forever poking and pushing the baby', says Tessa 'and I know I'm not always consistent in the way I respond. I know I should react calmly and firmly but my emotions often get in the way because I want to protect the little one, and then I scream at him. The other day he pinched her really hard and I just grabbed him and shut him outside the room, then spent the rest of the day trying to make it up to him. I really could have hit him, which makes me feel terrible.'

'Behaviour like this is incredibly common,' reassures Dr Stephen Briers.

> But you've got to stop it happening. In the heat of the moment pinching or prodding is an unacceptable behaviour like any other and so it has to be stopped. If it's minor, try distraction, but, if harm is being done, you need a clear signal that it should not happen again. You have to let him know that pinching the baby will not be tolerated, by showing that there is a consequence for that behaviour, whether you choose time out, or a naughty step, or another sanction.

Some people feel uncomfortable about using time out (where the child is put in a safe place with the door shut for the equivalent of one minute for each year of his life), but Dr Briers suggests that this is probably more effective than moving the baby away:

*If you move the baby away the toddler could feel
even more excluded. Time out should only be for
as many minutes as the child's age, so it's three
minutes for a three-year-old, no longer. After that
you can acknowledge the toddler's feelings. Make it
clear that you understand that he feels frustrated
but that hurting the baby is not an acceptable way
of showing it.*

A child of three or more can also be motivated to be kind
and helpful to the baby with a star chart, or a technique
like the 'pasta jar'. Each day starts with ten pieces of pasta
in the jar and every time your child does something good
or kind, he gets another piece of pasta added to the jar.
Any bad behaviour gets a piece removed from the jar. At
the end of the day the pieces in the jar can be counted up
and swapped for a small gift or treat, such as extra time
with you (preferably not food or sweets, which can create
an unhealthy connection between food and reward). This
will give a child a strong incentive to change his difficult
behaviour.

G is for guilty

A child who is adjusting to having a new sibling can become
quite adept at manipulating your emotions. Don't let her
confused or difficult feelings play you. She might be going
through a tough time adjusting, but hopefully you haven't
ruined her life. I remember feeling inexplicably guilty when
my daughter started crying, 'I want to go on holidays!', as
she sat with me and the new baby. As we had been 'on
holidays' shortly before the baby was born, I read this as a

clear desire to return to our previous state, unencumbered by her brother. But perhaps that was me putting a far more sophisticated spin on her feelings than her two-year-old brain could, and moments later she had moved on to something else.

'I felt like she was angry with me and rejecting me,' recalls Anna, whose daughter, Ruby, became uncooperative and tearful after baby Elinor was born.

> I sensed that she was jealous, but couldn't really articulate that feeling. One day she said to me, 'Mum, Elinor needs to go to hospital now.' I realized she meant to take her back. She looked so desperate, it made me feel guilty. I had been getting so cross with her and it wasn't really her fault.

An increasingly heated relationship with the eldest child can also foster guilt. Suddenly most of your interactions with him seem to be negative ones. If he's playing up more, it's easy to get into a negative cycle, where you're far more critical of him than you were before the baby came, and he in turn reacts to more telling off with more challenging behaviour. Since a child of two or more is already beginning to test your boundaries, the result can be explosive. But the danger is that this behaviour might make you less and less keen to spend time with him.

Equally, a toddler can be so demanding that you can end up feeling guilty about whether or not you're spending enough time focusing on the baby, particularly as he begins to grow and develop. Luckily the baby has never known it any other way and, so long as he's getting fed and changed when he needs it, will probably be more patient about waiting for attention.

'I did feel guilty because I preferred time with the baby,' recalls Anna.

> Ruby was so hard to please and seemed to use the slightest thing as an excuse for a tantrum. But it did help when I faced up to how Ruby was feeling, rather than just sweeping it away. 'This baby isn't much fun for you is she?' I said to her and she shook her head. I couldn't give her everything she wanted, but I could appreciate her point of view. After a while she seemed less touchy, so we weren't sparking off each other so much.

The baby is your friend

Although you can't prevent your elder child from feeling confused or put out by her sibling's arrival, there are things you can do as a parent to help promote a warm and loving relationship between them. Professor Judy Dunn's research into how sibling relationships develop found that engaging an older child's interest in the baby's care can have a vital impact: 'Our research shows that in families where the first child was interested and affectionate towards the baby the relationship continued to be loving and supportive for both children,' she says.

Studying many families over time, Dunn found that differences in the way the mother talked about the baby were linked to the quality of the relationship that developed between the siblings. What seemed to make a difference was when mothers talked about the baby as a person with needs, wants and feelings, and encouraged the older child to express his opinions too. For example, you might ask him why he thinks the baby could be upset, with questions such as, 'Do you think he's hungry? Shall we give him his bottle and see if he likes it?'. When the baby starts smiling, you can say, 'Look, the baby's smiling at you. He really likes you.'

When my third child was born I found it helped to engage his elder siblings by pretending that the baby could talk. I would do his voice, which would brag to them about all the exploits he got up to while they slept. My son and daughter would love to correct him, patiently reminding him that he was still a baby and couldn't possibly have a motorbike, fly to the moon or go ice-skating.

Making the baby fun and involving the older child can work well on all sides. The older child can enjoy learning how to play with a baby, and help with nappy changing, dressing or gently winding the baby. I found a very sweet moment on a home video, where my two-year-old daughter tries to soothe her grisly newborn brother. 'Oh, you're crying. Have you got a burp?' she asks him, with great curiosity, and taps on his back in a way she must have seen his father or me doing. Small children can be fascinated by all sorts of things about a baby: one mother even mentioned a new baby's yellow poo as being a great source of interest. You can also show the older child safe ways of touching the baby with comments such as: 'Your sister likes it when you tickle her feet'.

Trish, whose son Alex was vigorously attacking his brother, Tom, realized that this approach was an important one for her. 'I used to get Alex to help mix Tom's feed and then give him his bottle. It worked well to make him feel responsible,' she says.

Babies love floor shows; and, as the baby gets older, a child can quickly learn that playing with her is a great way to get your attention and praise. By about six months a baby will be able to laugh at the funny things her sibling does, and making the baby laugh can be a great boost to the older child.

Promoting a desire to help also means not overreacting to your child's enthusiasm. Rosie was horrified when four-year-old Tania grabbed baby Max from his cot and staggered down three flights of stairs, holding him like a rag doll. 'She looked so pleased with herself, telling me, "Mum, he was crying!"', Rosie recalls. 'My immediate instinct was to scream at her, but I knew that, if I was heavy-handed, she'd really resent it. And besides, it showed that she was caring for him. I just thanked her and grabbed him back as delicately as I could.'

The baby bites back

For most families things begin to calm down as the baby's first year passes, and the elder child gets more used to having a sibling around. The baby is a static creature who can be played with or ignored, depending on the older child's mood.

But then it all changes again, when the baby starts moving, and tensions can mount. As the baby expresses an interest in the toys and games of the older child, the issue of sharing rears its ugly head. Older children can be hugely frustrated by little ones meddling with precious toys; they need to learn that if they don't want to share toys, then they must keep them out of the younger sibling's way.

I can't remember much about the early days of my

own younger brother, who is two years younger than me, but I do remember a moment of overwhelming rage as he toddled across to my dolls' cot and clambered into it. Everyone else thought he looked cute, sitting there like a big dolly. I wanted to hit him.

As well as meddling, the previously passive baby can now become the aggressor. I was completely taken aback the first time my docile baby son toddled across the room and began raining blows on his elder sister with an outstretched palm. Her expression was priceless: she was so surprised that she simply stood there with a look of utter disbelief. For an older child who is used to being in control it can come as quite a shock that her younger sibling can make life miserable. Anna recalls a similar experience with her second daughter, Elinor, who started becoming aggressive at the age of two:

> She will just grab a handful of her sister's hair and yank it. And it's not even as if she has had something taken away from her – sometimes she just gets a glint in her eye and she'll make a point of crossing the room to do it. But Ruby [her four-year-old sister] doesn't retaliate. Sometimes I'll find Ruby in tears because Elinor's pulled a great clump of hair. I tell Elinor, 'No!' very firmly and move her away, but I don't know what else I can do. The worst thing is that she doesn't even seem to care about being told off.

Dr Stephen Briers warns that it's important not to let the younger child get away with this kind of behaviour. 'As soon as she's old enough to understand that something is not OK, it can be associated with a meaningful consequence for her,' he comments.

But it needs to be something immediate. Often just the tone of voice and an appropriate sharp rebuke will be enough. Or you can try holding her firmly in a restraint for a minute, to show that this behaviour is not acceptable. If the problem keeps recurring, you can consider putting her into time out for two minutes. It's also important to explain to the older child how to stop the little one from hurting her, without hurting the younger sibling back.

More babies...

While nothing can be so intense as the transition from one to two kids, it would be a mistake to assume that older children aren't going to mind the appearance of subsequent babies. When Susan told her elder children she was expecting a fourth child, the second said to her incredulously, 'But Mum, we don't *need* any more babies!' 'When I told my daughters, who were then ten and eight, that I was expecting twins, they both cried,' recalls Izzy. 'They love them now, but definitely they felt destabilized for a while by the idea of their world changing so dramatically.'

Much of the advice written for parents focuses on the reaction of the first-born to a second baby. 'It's fair enough to say that it does have more of an impact on the first-born,' notes Professor Judy Dunn. 'When a third is born, on the whole both get on with the third one. On the whole the first-born being displaced is a more powerful influence than the second one.'

But for the younger child who is about to be unseated as the baby, it can be a bitter blow. He might never have known life on his own with his parents in the same way that his elder sibling has, but he has enjoyed the security of being the baby. And perhaps because parents are beginning to feel like old hands by the time a third child is born, they make less fuss about the whole thing, leaving the previous youngest feeling overlooked.

Anthony, who is one of seven children, remembers very well how it felt when the next baby arrived. 'From the perspective of adulthood I do think there was a level of resentment that each youngest felt when a new baby came along and you were shunted from prime position,' he says.

When my third child was born, his three-year-old elder brother resolutely refused to acknowledge his presence. If he saw the baby in a room, he would walk out again. He then started to pay his new brother attention in a kind of creepy faux manner. 'Gee, you're sooooo cute!' he would say to the baby in an American accent. 'I *really* love ya.' I wasn't fooled by these declarations of love. But with hindsight, perhaps because we'd done this before, we were too relaxed about trying to involve him with his new brother. While his five-year-old sister was very busy with the baby, it was easy for him to take a back seat and limit his contact to a few wisecracking remarks.

Lisa's older children weren't fussed by the prospect of another baby. 'When I announced my fifth pregnancy the older two kids said 'Great! Now we can get a dog!' she recounts. 'I'd promised one when we'd had our last child'. Lisa and her friend Jean, who also has five children, think there's another added bonus for their eldest daughters, who are both the eldest of five kids. 'They are probably the least likely of all the teenage girls we know to fall pregnant early,' she says. 'They have no romantic ideas about looking after babies.'

The perfect age gap?

Having got through the ups and downs of my daughter's first year, I was horrified when people started asking me when I was planning the next baby. It hadn't even occurred to me, until I realized that, to aim for the so called 'optimal' two-year age gap, I would need to be pregnant again by the time my daughter was fifteen months – and that didn't leave much room for trying. 'You just can't risk waiting,' a helpful colleague told me. 'What if something goes wrong?'

Is there an optimal age gap for our children to enjoy a conflict-free relationship? The most common belief seems to be that two years is about right, and certainly you won't get much longer after having a first baby before people are asking about the next. But why should two years be the best gap? Although women who are having their babies later in life probably feel that they can't leave it too long, the notion of optimal spacing is still a relatively modern luxury. But as the tendency moves increasingly towards having just two kids, the pressure to 'get it right', perhaps, becomes more intense.

How we decide to space our children often has its roots in our own childhood, and all of us have different experiences to draw on. My older brother is just under two years older than me and my younger brother just over two years younger, and since we generally had a laugh together as children I can see that the two-year gap makes quite a bit of sense. But there was then a five-year gap before my sister was born, which helped me see the pros and cons of having a much younger child.

'I always felt that the six-year gap between me and my siblings was what made us less close, and made me more determined to have mine close together,' says Vanessa of her own childhood. But Lauren is at the other extreme. 'I deliberately decided on a four-year gap because I hated being so close in age to my older brother who was just sixteen months older than me. I always felt he was breathing down my neck and I wanted my kids to have more individual attention.'

A two-year gap means having a baby and a toddler at the same time, which can be exhausting. A two-year-old can be extremely demanding, and is going through his own developmental changes. To some extent, the length of gap comes down to personal choice: some people think getting all the nappies and sleeplessness out of the way in as few years as possible is the best way to go; others think you should wait until your first child is independent enough for you to really focus on number two. Some even like to get their first child off to school before thinking about the next.

Equally some parents think a larger age gap will minimize conflict, while others believe that an older child who has had more time on his own with them is going to be extra jealous. My mother, for example, says that three-plus is 'very well known for producing jealous, spiteful, possibly damaging behaviour against the baby'. Some experts apparently 'recommend' a four-year gap in order to give your children optimal attention, and the chance of better intellectual development, while other experts think children of similar ages will play better but compete more. In terms of immediate reaction to the birth of a sibling, there are some studies which suggest that children aged between two and five have a harder time adjusting than those aged less than twenty-four months, perhaps because the under-twos have less cognitive development.

But Professor Judy Dunn thinks the size of age gap is something that troubles parents more than it does the children. 'Mothers worry about it because it's one of the things that they can have a bit of control over, up to a point,' she says. 'But I found that a five-year-old can be just as disturbed and upset by a new sibling as an eighteen-month-old.' Generally she seems to have found that differences in the quality of the relationship were not linked to the age gap. 'On the whole I found that the age of the child when a sibling was born did not explain much of the difficulties in their relationship. It affected how they showed it at the time, how they reacted in terms of needs from their mothers – little ones wanting more attention, big ones behaving worse – but in terms of overall adjustment it didn't make that much difference.'

In the meantime, of course, all sorts of other things are going to come into play when we think about adding another child to the family: circumstances, age, finances and, of course, fertility are all going to play a part. And life isn't always straightforward. After a problem-free first pregnancy and the birth of her daughter, Freya, Sue planned for a two- to two-and-a-half-year gap before her next baby. But it was only when she lost the next pregnancy that she discovered that she was the carrier of a genetic condition. 'When I lost the first baby I was determined to get on and have another as soon as possible,' she recalls. 'I was worried about the gap between the kids – God knows why, possibly conditioning.'

But disaster struck a second time, and Sue was told that she only had a 50/50 chance of giving birth to a healthy baby. 'Suddenly panicking about age gaps took a back seat. My concern was whether I was ever going to be able to have another baby at all. I had never ever contemplated having an only child and that became a huge issue for me.'

Thankfully the next pregnancy was healthy and Sue's son Nicholas was born a full five years after his sister. So far the gap has worked well for Sue, who now says:

> I don't even think about the age gap now and I wonder why I got so worried about it. It doesn't ever bother me. Freya and Nicholas play together so well, and she is fantastic with him. I can't believe how lucky I am. So when I hear people ask, 'What's the best gap?' or 'I'm planning another when the baby is two,' I just think, well, it doesn't always work like that.

Small age gaps

Small age gaps seem to provoke intense reactions. 'Are people with small age gaps just boasting about their fertility?' asked a parenting message board; but for some parents it isn't part of life's grand plan. Eda has twelve months between her sons Ethan and Rory. 'I was devastated when I found I was pregnant again,' she says.

For most of Ethan's first year I was pregnant and exhausted. Then the first year of Rory's life was a complete blur too, one feeding, one teething. But now when I see all my friends struggling with a newborn and their toddler is giving them hell I feel really glad I did it that way. There were no adjustment problems because they could never remember it any other way. They play together brilliantly, though they can fight a lot too.

Is there any truth that children who are born closer together get along better? Certainly two children who are close together in age are more likely to share similar interests, toys and friends, but the rivalry between them can also be intense. They can fight when they're together, but hate to be apart. Eda clearly recognizes this description. 'Rory finds Ethan maddening at times. It can get very heated. But when Ethan went away to his Nan for the night Rory really pined. He was like a lost soul. It was touching.'

Lesley, whose two boys Ben and Sam are just fifteen months apart and now aged nine and ten, finds their closeness in age causes problems. 'Just from a biological point of view, at each stage of their development, everything is happening really close together,' she observes. 'It has made it really difficult for them to carve out their own identity and space.'

Big gaps

There's no doubt that people with large age gaps feel sensitive about other people's assumptions: that later children weren't planned, or must have different fathers, or that the mother couldn't bear her children growing up, or didn't want to go back to work. Far more likely causes of large age gaps might be either fertility problems – with time spent in having IVF or perhaps many miscarriages – or financial reasons, with some people holding off until they feel more able to support another child. Or sometimes people simply find they want another child.

But there are benefits. Research suggests that children over the age of five are less likely to react badly to the birth of a sibling, although of course that doesn't mean repercussions won't be felt later. A longer gap also might give the parents more time for one-on-one attention with the youngest, while older children are at school.

An older child can embrace the idea of a baby more easily, and is more likely to be a willing helper. Freud, for one, thought that an elder girl sibling's maternal instinct would kick in once she reached the age of five, the age my daughter was when her second brother was born. She loved the idea of having a baby in the family, planned to call him 'Cutie Pie Darling', and made him paper mobiles and cards. I found one the other day: 'To the bestest baby in the world.' She loved to hold him, help bath him, stick a dummy in his mouth and later a bottle.

But just because a child is older and better able to grasp the notion of having a baby doesn't make the transition an easy one. Grace's mother had had repeated miscarriages after her, and Grace was nearly eight by the time her sister was born. 'I used to pray every night on bended knee for a brother or sister,' remembers Grace. 'But when she came, my nose was thoroughly out of joint. I can remember leaning over the cradle and being *so* upset. I was told about the softness of her fontanelle and then I hit her there with a rattle. Obviously not that hard, but I was so angry with her.'

When a second sister joined the family two years later, Grace felt even more left out. 'By that point I might as well have not existed,' she recalls. 'All family activity was about the little ones and the logistics of them left me frustrated. Imagine how I felt with activities like going to feed the ducks when they were five and three and I was thirteen. We are very close now, but it only really happened after they'd left home.'

There's clearly less likelihood that children with a big age gap will play together. My own sister is seven years younger than me, and although we played together quite a lot when she was small, I can see now that it wasn't always easy for her. 'I often felt left out because you had your own games,' my sister remembers.

> *And even when you were being nice to me, there was still an undercurrent that you could steer the story whichever way you wanted to. You were so much older than me in terms of development, so I was never going to have the same mastery of language. You could get me with sarcasm that could leave me in a helpless rage.*

Managing the needs of different age groups can also be hard. Vicky had her fourth child when her next youngest was already nine and her older two were fast approaching their teens. 'Although they love their little sister, they don't really play with her, which means she gets more spoiled by me,' she reflects.

*We can never be in one place that pleases
everyone, and she does restrict a lot of what
we can do as a family. If we're in the kiddie
playground, the elder ones are going mad and the
other mothers are glaring at them. If we do what
the big ones want, then the toddler whinges. And
we have terrible telly wars – the little one wants
CBeebies and they want MTV. Sometimes I get
teenage strops and toddler tantrums at the same
time. I do have two great babysitters when I need
one, but in some ways I know it would have been
easier if I'd had her sooner.*

Casey, who was just sixteen when she had her first son
Lee, had a sixteen-year gap before her second son, Darrell,
was born. 'They developed a really lovely relationship,' she
reflects, 'though Lee was so embarrassed when I said I was
pregnant, just the thought of what I'd been doing was more
than he could stand. And he would never push the pram for
me in case he either got mistaken for a teen dad, or my toy
boy.'

The ideal number of children

Users of the internet-based mother's forum *Mumsnet* post
frequent debates about the optimum number of children.
Some parents think two is too neat. Some think three causes
too much friction, and that 'three's a crowd' means someone
is always going to be left out. Others think three means,
'There's always someone else to play with – the dynamics
of three work really well.' Proponents of four argue that the
siblings can divide into two camps, but that it might not suit

if you value your peace or privacy. 'Three is hard work,' said one mother. 'But four is drudgery'.

Research suggests that the parents' own background frequently has an impact on their own family size. It certainly seems that people who come from large families can see the benefits more clearly of having large families themselves. As both my husband and I are one of four, it is surprising, then, that we stopped at three, though I often say I would have had four, if I had been younger and richer (and he says, if we did, he'd be off). But then my father was an only child, so perhaps a lack of siblings can equally spur you the other way.

Clearly there are pros and cons to each sibling combination. Sometimes the limitation of having just one sibling to lean on can seem severe, especially if you don't get on. 'That was the worst thing for me about not liking my sister,' says Steph. 'The realisation that we were stuck with each other, and it's not going to get any better than this. That feeling of "Is this it?" has never gone away.'

In any case there are no certainties when you're planning your sibling brood. Matt and Mandie thought they would try for baby number three – and got triplets. 'We were just planning on having three and ended up with five kids,' says Mandie. 'So we went from two to five in one leap. It was mad. I love them all, of course, but bringing up five kids in a three-bedroom house on a council estate is hard. Next time I'll have an au pair and an ironing lady!'

Ten and counting...

I recently heard a woman talking on a radio phone-in, describing her experiences as a member of a huge family as 'tantamount to child abuse. I got so little attention you could call it neglect,' she complained.

Huge families are relatively unusual nowadays but, as with many things relating to siblings, there doesn't seem to be a consensus on whether it makes for a tumbling, happy-go-lucky brood, or a bunch of kids fighting to the death for attention.

The writer Amanda Foreman claimed in a recent article:

> *Children in large families seem more relaxed around each other, more confident and independent because they do not have such an intense focus from their parents as those with only one sibling.*
>
> *Those with lots of siblings learn so much from each other, how to share everything, from toys to their parents' attention. Through the rough and tumble of family life, they learn how to negotiate and compromise. They grow up knowing they are not the centre of the universe, which can only be healthy.*

By contrast, Foreman felt that parents with only two children are more intense, loading them with their desires and dreams and pressurizing them to succeed.

Anthony, third youngest of seven children, sees it slightly differently: 'My sister's fiancé used to call us the piranhas: he felt that joining us at meal times was like having strips of flesh bitten off him by a frenzied school of attention-starved carnivores,' he recounts.

WE DON'T NEED ANOTHER BABY

*At our dinner table there'd be shouting across
each other and stealing food from the plates of
younger siblings. We learned to demand space,
demand attention. The large family dynamic didn't
suit shrinking violets. We fought and argued and
insulted each other as a form of sport – and if you
couldn't laugh at yourself you got no sympathy. A
large family with only two parents doesn't have a
lot to go around. We found it in other ways, partly
it seems by fighting with each other.*

It might have been a tough environment to grow up in, but
there were pluses too: 'All my siblings and I are good in a
crowd,' says Anthony. 'We are at ease meeting new people
and good at entertaining ourselves. Sometimes it did feel
like a battleground, but growing up in a big family was
never dull.'

CHAPTER TWO

I'm bigger than you

It would be nice to be able to think that you could predict how siblings were going to get on according to the laws of birth order. Certainly it is a topic, which sparks both fascination and controversy, and there are plenty of books and studies to be found on the subject. Birth order aficionados believe that your place in the family will affect your relationships, self-image and interactions with others throughout childhood, and that it is at the root of much sibling conflict.

But it can be hard to apply what we know about birth order as a precise science. While there are undoubtedly some links between the way children behave and their place in the family, birth order is not necessarily an accurate predictor of how they will develop, or what their relationships will be like, or indeed whether children are going to get on. The TV experiments I've seen where experts tried to guess a group of people's birth positions from information about their adult lives were dismal failures. Children's personalities, the way they are parented and the social and economic circumstances of the family – in particular major events, such as illness, death or divorce – are all just as likely to have an impact on how they turn out.

Nevertheless, it can be both interesting and revealing to think about yourself and your children in the context of your birth order. I'm a middle child, sandwiched between two boys, and then with a younger sister following that, so I can happily ascribe some of my youthful unwillingness to conform to that positioning; however my elder brother doesn't seem like a domineering eldest child at all. Meanwhile my husband was the adored youngest child of four, and seems to have never lost that sense of specialness; his older brother still refers to him, not entirely warmly, as 'golden boy'. As for my own children, I know I expect more of my eldest at times than I do of her brothers. I know I baby the youngest. And I know that I often put down some of my middle child's difficulties in negotiating family life to being 'the middle child'.

While it can be an illuminating way of looking at things, it's also important not to lock children into their birth position. Every position has its advantages and its disadvantages, but ultimately what's going to matter more for each child is being individually appreciated, rather than how he or she appears in relation to his or her siblings.

It's tough being the eldest

According to the birth order theory, first-born children are more likely to be competitive, dominant, assertive, self-assured and do well at school. The eldest child will have a strong desire to please her parents, and might try to emulate them. Because the eldest child gets the early years of intense focus from her parents before any siblings come along, parents might continue to invest more time and effort in her achievements; consequently she might also feel pressurized or that she is only valued if she performs well. She might be conscientious and even perfectionist, but also controlling. She can be emotionally intense or bossy, and insist on doing things 'her way'.

Certainly in some families the dominance of the eldest can be long lasting. William didn't realize, until his brother Shaun stood up and made the best man's speech at his wedding, that Shaun felt he had lived in his brother's shadow. 'He said he'd spent his whole life looking up to me,' recalls William. Nonetheless William was unrepentant. 'I wasn't interested in him when we were children,' he admits. 'He was constantly snapping at my heels and I was pushing him away. He wanted to do whatever I was doing – and I didn't want him doing it with me. He always wanted to be my brother, whereas I didn't share the same feelings about him.'

Somehow these issues were never resolved between the two brothers until they became adults. 'I didn't realize that he still carries a lot of resentment about how I dominated him,' says William. 'Maybe because we were boys it made it worse.'

While a domineering eldest can crush a younger child, it's important to watch out that an eldest child doesn't get blamed automatically for things that go wrong. My daughter often accuses me of this: 'You always blame me just because I'm the eldest!' Equally, Mandie's eldest of five kids, eleven-year-old Shelby, frequently gets into trouble for fighting with his nine-year-old brother Tannar. But with six-year-old triplets in the family as well, Shelby feels that he always gets the blame. 'It cuts both ways,' says Mandie. 'He's often the one who picks the fights because he's in a bad mood, but I know that it's sometimes hard for him. I do feel sorry for him. He was three when his brother was born, and then five when the triplets came along, and he didn't get a lot of attention.'

One pitfall is to expect a lot from older children but not give them the privileges in return. If an eldest child doesn't feel that there are advantages that come with age, he might take out his resentment on the younger kids. It can help by making an effort to include him in a special treat, or by giving him responsibility to do particular errands, which will make him feel that he is being recognized for being the elder.

Mandie is aware that Shelby does enjoy greater privileges than the other children. 'I know I do put a lot on him,' she says. 'He understands that he's the eldest and that's how it is. But then he also gets a lot more back. All our Sundays revolve around his football training; he gets to go up to the shop for me. But from the point of view of attention he does get more time with us on his own. Because he's the eldest he gets to stay up later and that's his special time.'

It's easy to slide into taking it for granted that older children are going to help out and act as unpaid backup. Although it's hugely useful to use the eldest child as our eyes and ears, and an extra pair of hands, she can't be made to feel accountable for the younger child's behaviour. My nine-year-old daughter sometimes gets her four-year-old brother dressed and ready, but, if I rely on her too much to do this, it can backfire. He might decide not to cooperate or she might lose her temper and, before long, they are lashing out at each other.

As an older child I was often relied upon to help look after my sister, who is seven years younger than me. I used to walk her up and down the corridor to help keep her quiet and often played with her as a toddler. But I didn't always feel like being responsible and sensible, and sometimes would provoke her instead. I recognize the same feelings in my eldest child now. It's lovely when she wants to help, but too much expectation makes her feel frustrated and likely to snap.

Eldest children are also the family pioneers: first to go to school, do exams, and confront the challenges of teendom. They are likely to be treated more strictly, and might have to endure far greater restrictions than their younger siblings will at a similar age.

While experts suggest that the first-born responds better to adult company than other children do, it is important not to turn him into a mini grown-up. For Grace, being much older than her two sisters meant that she always felt she got the raw deal. 'Our mother wasn't that well after she had them, which meant I had to grow up fast,' she reflects.

By the time my sisters were at school my father was using me as a confidante for all sorts of problems, stuff I shouldn't have had to listen to, like his affairs, and money worries. My sisters were always protected from family problems I felt, and it wasn't until I moved away in my late twenties that I managed to break the whole family dynamic of them being the protected babies and me being the big girl.

Similarly Steph felt that her sister, being the younger, 'more immature one, meant that she got away with stuff. She was let off a lot of things that I'd had to fight for. The oldest breaks down the barriers and then the younger romps through without even noticing.'

Middle-child syndrome

Some birth order experts maintain that they can always spot a middle child; something to do with the massive chip firmly implanted on his shoulder, perhaps. Certainly the typical view is that the middle child suffers from a permanent state of injustice, and feels neither as loved nor as wanted as the elder and younger children. He has neither the status of the eldest nor the perks of the youngest, feeling like 'piggy in the middle' or the odd one out. He feels that he gets less time, attention and even financial resources from his parents; to get your attention, he might lurch between rebellion, on one hand, and trying to please on the other. While first-borns are more likely to do well in school, middle children are apparently more likely to drop out, earn less, have teenage pregnancies and even be led into criminality. Clearly I got off lightly.

But on the plus side, the middle child benefits from being both an older and a younger sibling; he's got a leader to show him the way, and a follower to look up to him. This can help middle children become good negotiators, and they will often have a strong sense of fair play and justice.

'I definitely felt left out as the middle child,' says Susan, 'which is one reason why I decided to have a fourth child myself.' She recalls:

My older sister did everything first, had all the responsibility, and all the power. My little sister played the baby role to the hilt with tantrums and throwing her weight around. I don't think I had a clear sense of my place in the family and possibly for that reason I became the family clown because acting like an idiot is a great way of getting attention. It's something I still do as an adult.

But not everyone shares this negative view. Keith, who is the middle of three boys, found he got the best of all worlds:

My mum was less stressed with me than she was with my first brother. I thought number two was a good place to be: less of the pressure my older brother had, less of the feeling like 'last man in' of number three. Both my brothers always wanted to play with me, so it felt like I was in control.

'My sister was the middle child,' says Douglas. 'She spent so much time complaining about favouritism, and my parents got so worried that she felt left out that she actually got all the attention!'

Experts suggest that a middle child will need extra reassurance, and that you will need to make time for him, away from the pushy eldest and attention-hogging youngest. The middle child might feel that the oldest child gets praise for being able to help, and the youngest for achieving new skills. Encourage his interests and ask his opinions. He might also need extra praise.

My middle child is prone to putting himself down so that when I praise him, he bats it straight back at me. 'You did that piece of writing really well,' I might say, only for him to reply, 'No I didn't, it's rubbish.' It's as if he needs an extra layer of reassurance, perhaps because he genuinely does feel that he can't measure up to his competent older sister. But, if I give him responsibility or ask him to look after his younger brother, he is just as capable of rising to the challenge.

In families of four children, middle children occupy slightly different positions. 'I would say four does minimize the middle-child syndrome,' says Susan. 'Although they all get on well, my eldest two are very close, which means that if they go off together, number three still has number four. But in any case, any pairing works to some extent. Everyone always has someone.' In my own family of four kids, it seemed like my eldest brother was often allied to the youngest, my sister, while the middle two, my younger brother and I, were the troublemakers. But these pairings were always shifting, with elder brother often playing divide and rule, and manipulating my younger brother and I to turn on each other.

Birth order experts also make the distinction between the middle child in a family of three, and the middle child of a larger family. Children who are in the middle of large families might complain that they get clobbered at both ends of the spectrum: when there are chores for the big kids, they are one of them; but when there are fewer privileges for the little kids, they're one of them too. Middle children of large families might also be less competitive than their siblings – as their parents don't have much time to give each child, middle children learn to cooperate to get the attention or status they want.

Mandie's middle child, Tannar, in between the eldest and younger triplets, has managed to find his own way of getting attention. 'He's a bit of a boffin,' says Mandie, 'so he gets his attention by doing really well at school. I also get him to read the little ones their bedtime stories, so he has some responsibility. But when I let him go to the shop for me, then he feels he's one of the big ones.'

Curiously families who have twins plus another child also report that they can have middle child syndrome. 'My older sister had to be the first to do everything and was always the boss,' says Ian, who is one of twins. 'But my twin sister, who is all of twelve minutes younger than me always acted the baby. So I had to be more independent. Maybe I made up for it a bit by being the only boy, but I always felt like I was left out, sandwiched between the two girls.'

It's tough being the youngest

Whether we think it's important or not, children are obsessed with birth order, and in my family the Number One insult is 'baby!' My children are acutely age-conscious and none more so than my youngest child. A while ago he came up with his own rather smart retort to anyone who might care to mention that he was a baby. 'You was a baby, ha ha!' he would scoff. There's not much you can say to that.

The textbook view of the youngest child is that he will be more creative, charming and affectionate than his older siblings. He will be less conscientious, and will happily compensate for being younger by stealing the spotlight from his siblings. Because parents will be pretty busy with their expanding family, he might feel less pressure from parental scrutiny, which can make him unconventional and more open to adventure.

Youngest children will develop social skills early on as they have siblings to learn from. But in other ways it might be easy to remain a baby, and mothers are prone to babying their youngest child. My youngest has been slow to discard the trappings of babyhood, because there was no new baby snapping at his heels to take over his cot, his buggy or his bottle. He can still persuade me to carry him, and demanded to use a buggy well into his fifth year, compared to his elder sister who never went in a buggy again after the age of two. His siblings tease him that he won't be able to wipe his bottom or put his shoes on by the time he starts school, and it's true. He is much more reluctant to become independent.

Many families describe their youngest child as the most chilled, the one who never has to bother, because everything comes to her. She might be used to the older children bringing her toys, and carrying her around. My daughter often carried my youngest son around on her back like a little monkey; no wonder he didn't walk until nearly eighteen months.

But some youngest children shrug off the trappings of babyhood as quickly as they can and will talk and walk earlier in a bid to keep up. My youngest son has a friend who is also the youngest of three; he freaks if you give him a plastic bowl or cutlery, insisting, 'I'm not a baby, I'm a big boy!' And there are some things that the baby might get far sooner than his siblings did. I would have baulked at letting my eldest child watch *Dr Who* at age three, but once the elder children are watching it, it's easy for the youngest to settle in for some unsuitable viewing without anyone really noticing.

He might be more indulged, but to be the baby is a mixed blessing. My own youngest often asks, 'Why do I always have to be last?' His perception is of being constantly pushed out of the way by the bigger children and of being on the receiving end of relentless putdowns: 'You're a baby, you can't do it.' He is perpetually reviewing the state of his privileges. 'When I am five, I will go to school,' he intones. 'When I am six, I will have a sleepover. When I am eight, I will have a guinea pig.' With elder brothers and sisters rolling out the ground rules, it must feel as if he has everything laid out for him. 'Why can't I have a Nintendo?' he demanded recently. 'Because I didn't get one until I was six,' answered his brother firmly, 'so that's when you have to get yours...' (except that the canny old baby managed to get his hands on the half-broken one his brother had discarded, and made that his own).

To redress that feeling of always being last, the littlest can go for attention-seeking wind-ups like throwing food across the table, or purposefully messing up things his older siblings are doing. He can also be manipulative. It's dawned on me over the last few months that my youngest child is incredibly provocative. He likes to light the blue touch-paper and then stand back, for example, by making a randomly provocative remark, then protesting vigorously when his siblings retaliate. And he is also highly vocal in making his displeasure felt, with screams designed to make you buckle just for a moment's peace.

The youngest child might sometimes trade on her baby status to try and get away with not pulling her weight around the house. It helps to give the youngest age-appropriate tasks and chores that will help reinforce the idea that she is an active participating member of the family rather than a baby. This might well improve her confidence in herself and help her feel that she can keep up with her elders.

THEY STARTED IT!

Older children often perceive the youngest as being allowed to get away with things, and this can cause friction. Lou recounts how her sister was always jealous of her status in the family as the youngest of four. 'She was always accusing me of "getting everything",' Lou recalls. 'It wasn't until we were in our early twenties that I was able to get her to see the other side of the coin: that I was always struggling not to be seen as the baby, and how hard that was at times for me. I think it made her realize, because we certainly got on much better after that.'

Youngest children can worship their older siblings and be confused by the inevitable rejection they suffer at times. They might feel overwhelmed and discouraged, and the sense that they can never catch up can lead to either passivity, or pushiness. They sometimes might need protecting, or support in standing up for themselves.

For thirty-two-year-old Julie, being the youngest meant having to push herself to the limit to keep up with her two brothers who were six and nine when she was born. 'I always had to "live up" to them,' she recalls.

I wanted to play with them but they were so much older that I had to really throw myself into things to be included. This meant some pretty unpleasant bullying. That was their 'prize' for having a tiny tot trailing after them the whole time. They would usually set me impossible tasks, so that I couldn't join in. They even got me to jump off a roof once. My main way of retaliating was actually keeping up. I would leap to the challenge and usually hang in there. It's made me into the competitive pest I am today.

Birth order research suggests that the youngest is least likely to be disciplined and least likely to stick to the rules. But there might be fewer rules in any case. My sister acknowledges that with siblings nine, seven and five years older than her, there were no real battles left to fight by the time she reached her teens. 'What was there left to do by the time I got there?' she asks. 'The bar for rebellion was so much higher that I felt I didn't need to bother.'

Twins – double the trouble?

Today, twins are a common occurrence: there are six sets at my children's small primary school. Even so, it's a relationship unlike any other, and to have twins gives you a touch of celebrity status. 'Twins mean constant attention,' observes Lucy, mother of now eleven-year-old twin girls. 'I could never get down the road with my twin buggy without someone stopping me.' 'People can't resist commenting,' agrees Nora, who has identical five-year-old boys. 'I'm always being told how lucky I am. But the truth is, it can be very intense. Twins are relentlessly hard work.'

Apart from the huge workload of having two babies at the same time, the twin relationship can be a powerful one for parents to deal with. Although twins can be very close, they will also know better than anyone how to wind each other up, and twins can be particularly volatile. They can also present a formidable force against others. 'They often gang up against me,' admits Lucy. 'Even when they were small, they would undermine my authority. If I ever tried to punish one, the other would always tell me to let her sister off.'

As with any other siblings, the temperament of individual twins will have a lot to do with how well they get on, and it's certainly not a given that they are going to be devoted to each other. Nursery teacher Nicola recalls how her relationship with her own twin, a boy, was not especially close. 'We always did different things,' she recalls. 'I wish that we could have been closer but it just didn't turn out that way.' She has seen at first hand at the nursery school where she now works how much twin relationships can vary:

> *There are four sets of twins of a similar age there and they are so different. There is one set that is absolutely inseparable. They hold hands all the time and don't talk to anyone else. I can see that one constantly holds the other back. Then there's another pair who are much more outgoing, and they hardly bother with each other at all.*

While parents may not be able to influence how well their twins get on, making sure that each is recognized as an individual and looking for the positives in each child can help. Twins particularly suffer from being labelled and compared; research has also found that twins receive less praise, perhaps because parents don't want to risk singling one out over the other when they are doing the same things. It's important to show each twin that they are appreciated for themselves, whatever their interests or aptitudes.

Lucy recalls how she started thinking about establishing her twin daughters' individual identities even before they were born:

I went to a talk at the hospital, and learned not to do things like dressing them the same or calling them 'the twins'. I also learned not to give them names that sound alike, say, Cherry and Jerry, or wildly different names like, say, Cordelia and Zoe, because then one would take longer, both to say and to learn to write her name, so would feel at a disadvantage.

Even forearmed, Lucy has found treating her twins as separate people hard work. 'It's tempting to compare them,' she admits, 'I have to bite my tongue all the time. I try as much as I can to allow them to be the individuals they are and help them develop separate friendships.'

Twins can feel that they have to exaggerate their differences to establish their own identity. 'Minnie and Kate get very cross if you muddle them up,' says Lucy. 'Even so, people typecast them as a pair. When Kate was in trouble at school, the teacher asked her, "Was Minnie involved in this?" as if one being naughty automatically meant the other would be, too.'

Many schools advise putting twins in separate classes, to allow them to develop their own friendships and abilities, but Lucy, whose twins are just finishing primary school, now wishes she had put them into separate schools: 'Even in separate classes they've been compared *all* the time,' she says; 'I felt that the school pigeonholed them as one being much cleverer than the other. They recently sat 11+ and, when I asked for their scores, there was actually only one point between them.'

Minnie and Kate are now going to separate secondary schools. 'No one will know they're twins which is brilliant,' says Lucy. 'They can be themselves and not be compared.'

Of course, to twins the existence of a double is simply the norm. Three-year-old Sophie – one of boy/girl twins – was incredulous when she met another girl of her age, and discovered that she didn't have a twin. 'Where's her brother?' she asked her mother. It had never dawned on her that not everyone arrives with a ready-made sibling.

However, siblings of twins can feel that they get the short straw; for elder children, the arrival of twin siblings can leave them feeling completely upstaged, while younger siblings might feel that they can never live up to this unholy alliance.

Nora admits that she struggled to give enough attention to her elder daughter Naomi, who was three when her twin brothers were born:

> *It can be so hard to look after the older child's needs when you've got twin babies. Even now that Sol and Benji are five, it sometimes feels like the twins get 90 per cent of my time and Naomi gets the other 10 per cent. If you've got twins, you've got to draw on as much support as possible, in any way you can. On Saturdays, I get my husband to take the boys out and no matter how many other things I've got that need doing, I spend an hour with Naomi doing what she wants to do. Hopefully that helps keep the resentment at bay.*

They're leaving me out – sibling alliances

If you've got more than two children, the chances are that at times they're going to gang up against each other, so that someone gets left out. This can be particularly bad in families of three children, where it's not uncommon for the youngest child to ally with the eldest, thus leaving the middle child out.

My middle child constantly feels left out and angry, and at times my heart goes out to him. 'The other two have made a club and said that I can't join – membership is only for two,' is a common complaint. A popular technique when children are upset is to reflect their feelings (sometimes called reflective listening, see p 163), so I asked 'How does that make you feel?' He replied, 'I'm sad and upset. If I'm with one of them, the other one always has to join in, but, when they're together, I'm not allowed to.'

'But they let you play Darling (a make-believe game of theirs) with them,' I pointed out. 'Yes,' he agreed, 'but I always have to be George, the poor friend who lives with a grumpy mother and is so poor he only gets 1p on his birthday!'

My attempts at coming up with solutions only seemed to make it worse. 'You know, you can ignore them,' I suggested. He harrumphed. 'Or go and find something else to do. Or you could spend some time with me.' He harrumphed again. That didn't appeal either. In truth it seems there's little I can do.

But all is not lost. Psychologists think that there are some advantages for children in having to deal with the cut and thrust of sibling politics. It not only teaches them how to deal with rejection, but also encourages them to work out how to make friends and influence people. It's dominate or be left out, which could stand them in good stead for adult life.

But is there anything parents can do to encourage children to play together? 'You can't force it,' observes clinical psychologist Dr Stephen Briers.

You can't force any three people – related or not – to get along, and there's nothing to be gained by trying to force the other two to embrace the outsider. His best bet is to initiate something that they can come and join, which will lead them off into something different. The only thing you can do is to suggest something where they have to collaborate and every member of the group has to play an indispensable role.

But it's also worth reminding children that patterns of alliance do shift. Just because it's like this now, doesn't mean it always will be. Perhaps the left out child can have a friend over to play at times to balance things out. But don't make too big a deal of it. There's a tendency for parents to feel that they have to make everything right for their kids, because it triggers uncomfortable feelings of their own. The message has to be about trying to normalize these things: it's not intolerable, you will survive.

The gender mix

While birth order can make a difference to how children interact with each other, gender is also going to play a part. Whether you have a mixed family or a single sex one, the gender line-up is likely to influence how the children get along. However, in terms of whether boys, girls, or a mixture, get along better, the evidence is contradictory.

Some studies suggest that sibling rivalry is worse between same-sex children who are close together in age. Some researchers think that families of girls are more peaceable than families of boys, but that mixed pairs get along best. But research by Professor Judy Dunn found the exact opposite: that during the early years children of different sexes get along worse.

'We found that with pre-school children the most quarrelsome combination was an older sister with a younger brother,' she comments. 'But other studies haven't found this and it may be that it changes over time. Broadly we found fighting to be more common between children of different sexes.' A first-born girl followed by a boy is the combination I have, with another boy thrown in for good measure, which, perhaps, explains why my children fight so much.

Single-sex families often have their own dynamics; research also suggests that children of the same gender may feel more intensively that they have to compete with each other. Boys can be more competitive physically, while girls can compete in a more verbal and catty way. Mixed pairs – if my own experience is anything to go by – will be a bit of each. But do brothers and sisters have different kinds of relationships with each other?

Sisters

Some recent works on sisters claim that the sister bond is particularly strong. According to Terri Apter, author of *The Sister Knot*, 'Our sister is our greatest champion and our greatest companion, but she's also our most deadly competitor'. She claims that while all children vie for attention and love from their parents, the rivalry between sisters goes deeper, 'because a sister threatens our place in the family and in the world.'

Where there are just two girls in a family the pressure seems to be quite intense. 'I knew from a very early age how important my sister was,' says Izzy, who recalls:

> *The love I felt for her, but also the sense of envy.*
> *She was my competitor, and I was threatened by*
> *everything she could do. That sense has never gone*
> *away. I sometimes think that, if I hadn't been trying*
> *so hard to be like her, I wouldn't have achieved the*
> *half of what I have done. The competitive spirit*
> *can be a positive thing. But for years I was jealous*
> *because I thought she was more pretty and popular*
> *than me. When we got older, I discovered that she*
> *felt overshadowed by me too.*

'We might fight like cat and dog, but it's just as easily all forgotten,' says Kirsty, now in her twenties. 'I quite often have an argument with my sister and decide we're not talking to each other, but then five minutes later we forget and someone goes, "Oh, have you seen that gorgeous handbag?" and that's it, fight over and long forgotten!'

For Steph, the fact of being sisters did not mean automatic bonding. Her sister, Margaret, is three years younger than her and in her opinion very selfish and self-centred. 'We used to fight about everything and were always jealous of each other,' says Steph.

> *I always wanted everything she had, and for whatever reason didn't think I was getting it. As an adult my sister has always disappointed me. The only time we really got on was when I lived abroad. I often feel she doesn't like me and I'd like her to; I feel rejected by her. But the bottom line is I might put myself out for her but I know that she wouldn't for me.*

Some people think that, while two sisters can be highly competitive, three is a magic number. 'Three sisters is a very positively powerful force,' agrees Grace, whose two sisters are ten and eight years younger than her.

> *We are especially close and whilst there is competitiveness at times this never bubbles over, which I believe is definitely because of the third sister. Whenever tensions arise, it's always between two of the three and the presence of the third diffuses the situation.*

> *It's impossible for me to imagine anything that could break us up and I'm certain that my ability to keep going is made easier by a firm feeling of safety, which having Alice and Helen around creates. I think that anything less or more would be too complex; somehow the triumvirate works as a stable and grounding force.*

Brothers

Is it a given that boys – especially those who are close in age – are going to fight more? Certainly it seems that boys are better able to act out their rivalry in physical combat. But that also means that brothers are most likely to inflict the worst violence on each other.

'My boys are eight and five and they fight dreadfully,' says Vanessa.

> *Charlie, who's five, seems to be determined to prove to Archie, the eight-year-old, that he can be as tough as him. So he'll just bug Archie, and then Archie loses it and lashes out. I dread it. Every time I hear those cries, I think, Oh God, he's really hurt him. I'm terrified that one day they will really hurt each other and I'll find them in a pool of blood.*

Alex's experiences suggest just how exhausting boy rivals can be. 'We were always hugely competitive,' says Alex, who was eighteen months older than his brother Tom.

> *We competed over everything. We were a nightmare for our mother: if we weren't playfighting, it was real fighting. For the first six years, I wanted to kill him. I tried to drown him in the bath. He swung a satchel at me and knocked me down the stairs. From the age of twelve, we competed for girls. We had our last proper punch-up when we were seventeen and eighteen. We're in our forties, but even now if you give us fifteen minutes and a ball, we'll be playing competitive catch. We're like magnets: we're either locked tightly together, or repelling each other.*

'I don't think anyone could have done anything about it,' reflects Tom.

> *We were close in age, both boys, and could both be a total pain. But he had the physical advantage. I remember feeling in fights that he was going to break my back or stop me from breathing, or that he was going to kill me. As a child I disliked him intensely. But there's not an ounce of resentment now. We still love competing. It's part of our ongoing narrative thing. Any game that one person wins is not a final result; it's part of the lifelong 80 million set game of tennis we're involved in.*

Similarly William and his younger brother, Shaun, were fiercely competitive:

> *Ours was a competitive family and on top of that we were all athletic, so the competition manifested itself in many ways. Our sporting competition would spill over into everything so that we were also competitive in a petty way. We fought something wicked. The irony was that we were really quite similar and we could have been good mates, but I think the competition got in the way. It wasn't until I'd gone to university that I realized I didn't need to be adversarial with him. He can still annoy me now, but in a healthy way.*

But Shaun also got his own back, as William remembers: 'He looked up to me as an older brother, because he was three-

and-a-half years younger than me,' says William. 'But then he grew taller than me and people assumed that he was the older brother. That really got to me and he revelled in that.'

CHAPTER THREE

It's not fair

If there's one thing that can fuel the flames of sibling rivalry, it's the issue of fairness. Like many others, my children are obsessed with it. They have a range of special noises to describe the feeling: 'Ahuhhhhh!' (starts high in ascending pitch, with open mouth and incredulous stare) expresses outrage that someone else has been shown what they see as preferential treatment. Whereas 'Owwwwwhh' tends to mean something along the lines of, 'I'm not happy – and that means it's not fair'; and then, 'Whaaaat?' just means general injustice.

'Dat's not fair!' my youngest child learned to say, long before he had any idea what it meant. One mother described to me how she keeps an imaginary 'Fair Book'. 'Whenever a child says, "It's not fair," we say, "That's another one for the Fair Book!" It's currently running at about 12,000 pages,' she told me.

Indeed the conviction that your siblings are getting one over on you can be a lifelong affliction, and one that parents apparently can never escape. 'My three children are in their forties, and they still keep a beady eye out for which of *their* children I'm being a better grandmother to,' says Professor Judy Dunn. 'And at Sunday lunch they'll still be looking to see who has the most roast potatoes.'

Of course, fairness operates on several different levels. All children are obsessed with what they 'get': pocket money, computer time, who has a friend round to play more often, the biggest slice of cake; with older children, it's money and freedom, or who's allowed to do more than the other. Then there's the issue of equality: while children might expect to get an equal portion of cake, it stands to reason that they will enjoy different privileges at different ages. 'I tell my kids they get everything the same, but not at the same time,' says Susan. 'So Ollie and Fred get to go to bed later now, and Jo and Lisa will go to bed at the same time when they're that age. They will get the same at the same age. But that doesn't stop the little ones from keeping up the chorus of "It's not fair".'

But beneath the constant demands for fairness, what children secretly would like is their parents' undivided love and attention all to themselves, which is why they strive so fiercely to get as much as they can. 'I'm the only one who gets told off, it's not fair,' my daughter often says. But when I asked her, 'So how would you make things more equal?' she answered, 'Give the boys away. Then I would get all the attention!'

Although she said it lightly, I felt there was a kernel of truth in there; each child seems to worry that you prefer his or her siblings. Every compliment, every reprimand, every moment of one-on-one attention seems to be monitored, noted and stored away. While it's easy to make light of it, we all know that the resentment that this sense of unfairness engenders can run very deep; for some children, the sense of having a raw deal can last a lifetime. So before you dismiss the usual cries of 'It's not fair' with a stern rebuke, it helps to try and ascertain what kind of fairness your child is really talking about.

He gets, I get

'We've got really hung up on this thing of buying our children everything the same,' says Tom of his two daughters Ella and Amy. 'It started with little things like cups and hair bands, but it's got to the point now where we buy presents for them on each other's birthdays. I know it's mad but now I'm not sure how to break it without World War Three breaking out.'

Some parents can be intimidated by their children's highly attuned sense of injustice, to the point where it becomes a tyranny. I confess that the last time I took my eldest two children to buy school shoes, my youngest wept so copiously for shoes with flashing lights that I ended up buying him a pair. Well, he needed new shoes soon anyway, I reasoned. The trouble is that, although our desire not to upset children is clearly borne of love, if you keep pandering to them, they miss out on a valuable lesson: that is, that you can't always have something just because someone else does.

'This idea of everything having to be the same can be harmful,' agrees clinical psychologist Dr Stephen Briers.

Kids have this idea they are entitled to equality, but just because they believe it doesn't mean you have to pander to it. Parents feel locked into the idea that they have to bend over backwards to keep their children satisfied. But actually children do better if you don't always give them what they want. It's good for them to understand the notion of turn-taking: it's your turn now, my turn later. It's not the same all the time.

My own children have an incredibly annoying habit of telling me what they think they 'get', which often involves upping the ante for good measure. 'He got two sweets?' asks my son incredulously. 'That means I get a friend to play.' 'Whaaat? She had two hours on the computer?' 'That means I get three!' Apart from telling them that I decide who 'gets', I try not to let myself be manipulated by the constant grumbling. Even if I buy a pair of socks and a new toothbrush for one, there are choruses of pain and injustice from those without new socks, and it's tempting to try and even things out every time I go shopping, to minimize the conflict. But I've realized that my children need liberating from their obsession with everything being the same, and have started to stick to my guns.

Some experts recommend that it helps to give some attention to what a child might be feeling at one of these moments when he hasn't 'got', and help reflect the feeling to him. So I tried it on my youngest after I had bought pyjamas for his elder brother: 'I understand that you're upset that I didn't buy you anything today. When you need new pyjamas, I will buy them for you,' I told him. He came bouncing in the next morning. 'Are we getting my new pyjamas today?' he asked brightly.' I need them now!'

But I treat them all the same

As parents we can marvel at how we can give birth to two, three or more human beings who can be so markedly different from each other in looks, taste and temperament. Not only do we expect these different beings to get along with each other, we remain convinced that we can and do treat them exactly the same.

But research suggests that this, in fact, is not the case; the reason children grow up so different apparently has more to do with how you treat them, than the hand nature dealt them. Developmental psychologist Professor Judy Dunn explored the theory that children growing up in the same house with the same parents live completely different lives. She concluded that many of the common family experiences are in fact different for each sibling. 'Siblings are treated differently by their parents and by their siblings, and even if their treatment seems to be similar, they may experience it very differently,' she says.

It also seems that many children perceive themselves as not being treated the same. One of the first major studies of siblings interviewed a large number of five- and six-year-olds. Two-thirds of the children reported that their mother favoured either them or their sibling, and only one-third said they were equally treated. First-born children, in particular, often felt that they weren't treated equally, and that their younger sibling either got away with more, or got more` attention, than them.

But kids always say that, don't they? Is it true? Most of us are fairly sensitive to the idea that we don't treat our children equally. Few of us will admit, publicly at least, that we have favourites or prefer the company of one child to another. But the evidence from several different sibling studies tells a different story.

In one US study, only a third of mothers reported feeling the same level of affection for both their children and only a third said they gave the same level of attention to both. Just over half of mothers reported feeling more affectionate towards their younger child (average age of four) while only 13 per cent said they felt more affection for their older child. In a similar UK-based study, a whopping 61 per cent felt more affection for the younger sibling (average age of six-and-a-half), and only 10 per cent preferred the older child.

Evidence from these studies shows that a mother behaves differently even to the *same* child according to his or her developmental stage. It stands to reason that you don't speak to your five-year-old in the same way as you do to your one-year-old; but, when a child is small and needy, you also might be a lot more attentive to him than when he's at a much more confrontational stage. If that confrontational child witnesses you being attentive to his now smaller and needier brother, then the sense of difference – to which children are clearly sensitive – can increase. Professor Judy Dunn thinks that witnessing such differential behaviour can have a huge impact on a child.

Dunn's research has backed up the notion that children are acutely sensitive to how their parents treat them. She found that very early in childhood 'children perceive differences in how they are treated and frequently mind very much about those differences...' She suggests that 'differences in their parents' affection, interest, expectations and respect...are the significant influences on children's development, rather than more general aspects of their parents' personality or attitudes.' She also found a child's awareness of differential treatment starts very young: children as young as fourteen months will monitor the relationship between their mother and siblings, and learn to interrupt or draw attention to themselves with increasing skill.

But Dunn acknowledges that it is very hard to treat different children exactly the same. 'It's a conundrum,' she says. 'When they are different ages, how can you treat them exactly the same? They react differently to you, have different needs, it's a fantasy for psychologists to say treat them the same. Simple rules of thumb don't work.' What's important, she thinks, is to remember how sensitive children are to this perceived injustice, and to strive, wherever possible, for 'differential appreciation' rather than 'preferential treatment'. In other words, appreciate each child for whom she is, and look for the individual qualities in everyone, in as non-partisan a way as you can manage.

Why the preference?

So what makes us treat children differently? Often personality differences between children play a large part. Because children behave differently, you might react to them differently, which children can easily perceive as favouritism.

You might have one child who knows how to push your buttons or is challenging; he might find himself locked in a vicious circle where you don't like his behaviour and, as a result, find any number of reasons, even unintentionally, for spending less time with him. While you might not actually love your easy-going child more, it stands to reason that the child who moans at you, or is harder to please, is going to be less pleasurable to be around. Alternatively, his bad behaviour might lead you to get the kid gloves out.

'My brother still expects to be treated differently,' says Julie of her grown-up elder brother, now in his mid-thirties.

*He is stupidly good-looking and I think my mum
has a soft spot for him. But we do treat him
differently because none of us can cope with his
temper. He is still the only member of the family
who doesn't help with washing-up or household
stuff. My parents would rather ignore his
behaviour than have a bigger scene on their hands.*

Teresa is one of those rare mothers who is able to admit
that she doesn't treat her children the same, 'Dominic has a
very strong personality, is incredibly stubborn and assertive
and likes to get his own way,' she says of her nine-year-old
eldest child. 'He has to try harder to gain my attention and
will act up accordingly. I do discipline him more, because he
gives me more trouble than his brother and sister.'

Teresa ascribes the difference in the way she feels
about Dominic to his behaviour towards his brother,
six-year-old Cameron, who was born with some health
problems. She is convinced that Dominic bullies his brother,
although she is well aware that Cameron 'is not the innocent
I once thought he was; he will deliberately cry when he is
not getting his own way.' Nevertheless, she says, 'My view
of Dominic has been affected by how he and Cameron
get along. Dominic, I think, is insecure and gets comfort
from asserting himself over his brother.' Her certainty that
Dominic is a problem child has created something of a
vicious circle. 'I do love Dominic but he is very difficult to
parent. I repeatedly tell him that I don't like his behaviour
and I think this has translated to a negative view of himself,'
Teresa reflects. Perhaps, unsurprisingly, she also reports
that Dominic 'likes to compare himself to Cameron and is
very competitive'.

Differences in character seem to play a large part here; but it's not unreasonable to suppose that the more Dominic perceives himself to be the disfavoured child, the more he is going to display the behaviour that his mother doesn't like. While there isn't a lot you can do to change a child's temperament, it might be possible to improve a child's difficult behaviour by making sure she doesn't feel at a disadvantage. If anything, the more difficult a child is, the more she will need plenty of positive attention, to show her that she is getting exactly the same treatment as the other children. Meanwhile an 'easy' child might be getting away with more because he seems so compliant, which could be fuelling a sibling's sense of injustice.

The important thing is to try and minimize the sense of disfavour as much as possible. Research has found that adults who report having a favoured sibling can lack confidence, be more prone to anxiety and depression and suffer from a sense of inferiority. Professor Judy Dunn's research also points to direct links between different levels of maternal affection or discipline, and anxiety, or behaviour problems, in children. She found that, in families where the mother controlled the older child much more than the younger sibling, the older child was likely to show relatively high levels of problem behaviour; and that meant more fighting, too. Being treated differently was not only reflected in the children's feelings about themselves, but was also linked to conflict between the siblings.

Whether it is the child's behaviour that leads to the different treatment or the different treatment that causes the behaviour is a moot point. 'Of course it can be the child's behaviour, which contributes to the differential treatment,' says Professor Dunn. 'One child is often much easier to live with and be affectionate towards.' If that's the case, Dunn thinks it's vital, however hard it might be, that you don't show it. 'You may have to simply grit your teeth and not lavish all your affection on the one who loves you back.'

Be alert to favouritism

Any one of a variety of things can affect how you feel about a child: her position in the family, her outlook on life or her abilities. A child who has developmental or health problems might make you feel more protective. A child who is a difficult baby might get a completely different start in life with you than a child who is good-natured and restful. Despite your best intentions, you might unknowingly be giving preferential treatment to one child over another.

Teresa ascribes some of her stronger feelings for her younger son to his having had an easier birth, and more immediate bonding. She also finds him easier to be around. 'I think we are on the same wavelength and we relate to one another and have the same sense of humour. I identify strongly with his character and personality,' she says of her favoured child, Cameron.

'My favourite depends on who's being the nicest,' jokes mother of five, Mandie. But she also knows how difficult it can be not to disfavour a more demanding child, like her eldest son, Shelby. 'I can go for a couple of days when Shelby comes up to me and puts his arms around me and tells me he loves me,' says Mandie of her eldest child. 'Other days he's so moody I just can't stand to be near him: all that scowling and grunting. That's one reason why he spends a lot more time with my husband.'

My daughter has what could best be described as a

feisty temperament; she's not afraid to push boundaries or to challenge the way we treat her. She can be fantastic company and it goes without saying that I, and her father, adore her, but the combination of her character and her position as eldest child mean that there are more likely to be fireworks between us than with the other children. She often perceives this as favouring her brothers. 'You're always telling me off!' she will yell at us. 'You never tell the boys off.'

In fact, her strength of character and refusal to comply mean that she is actually very good at garnering attention from us, which the other children can in turn perceive as favouritism. The combination of my lively daughter, and the time and attention that my youngest child has taken during his baby years means that my middle child has often spent more time with his father. I have to make a conscious effort to spend more time with him to even things out. I know that to keep accusations of favouritism at bay, I need to make an effort to notice his positive qualities and give praise for his endeavours. Even small things, such as a trip to the shops or ten minutes' chatting, can make a difference.

Gender can make a difference, too, and it's worth watching out that you don't fall into stereotypical expectations. 'My dad was quite open about the fact that he was disappointed to have a daughter first,' says Neela. 'My younger brother was always his favourite. Now that we are adults, they still seem to treat him like some sort of golden boy.' My own family of two boys and two girls was also rather prone to boy-centricity. 'The boys' were often referred to with approval as some sort of entity in a way that 'the girls' never were. There were photos taken of three generations of males grouped together, but not of females. And there was approval for male-type activities, such as rugby, cricket and blokey drinking. It left me with an uncertain sense about the value of girls.

If there is a much younger child in the family, an older child might also feel that the baby is getting different and favoured treatment. It might seem unfair to an older child if a baby grabs things, pokes her finger in his eye or trashes his toys, but is apparently too young to appreciate what she is doing. 'You let her get away with everything just because she's little...' is a familiar cry. It's important to listen to these complaints and point out that the older child would have done very similar things when he was little, but that you understand how annoying such things can be.

But it feels *unfair*

Children are acutely aware of anything that might look like favouritism, and they love to test the waters too. When my daughter declares, 'You love the boys more than me,' my immediate reaction, like many others, is to reply defensively, 'Don't be silly, I love you all the same.'

But experts suggest that, if a child *feels* you are treating him unfairly, whether it is true or not, you need to pay attention to those feelings. Instead of replying, 'I love you all the same', you need to find ways of showing each child that he is loved uniquely and that you value him for himself, by saying, 'There's only one of you'.

'If a child says, "You love so and so more", never say, "It's not true", because that will force a defence mechanism to kick in,' advises psychotherapist Julie Lynn-Evans.

He won't believe you. How awful is it to grow up in a family feeling like you're second best? If it really isn't true, the best thing is to say, 'I'm sorry you think that, tell me what it is that makes you say it. I hear that you're angry and it makes me sad. What shall we do together to try and work this one out?' You need to take it seriously but don't give the child any power. It doesn't mean he's allowed to behave badly or hit someone.

I decided to put this to the test. My elder son asked me (in a very grumpy voice) who my favourite was. I asked him, 'Why do you say that? Do you feel like I have a favourite?' He said he thought it was his younger brother, 'because he's the littlest'; then came his older sister, 'you're medium with her'. 'And what about you?' I asked. 'I just get grump grump grump!' came the reply. 'You know I don't have a favourite,' I told him. 'You're my very special boy and there's only one you in the whole world.' He harrumphed at me and said, 'It doesn't feel like that.' But I could tell from his expression that he was pleased. 'So what makes you feel like that?' I persisted. 'Oh nothing,' he said airily. 'I just wanted to know.'

Keeping rivalry at bay

'Children become rivals when there's a general lack of love in the house,' says psychotherapist Julie Lynn-Evans. 'Perhaps the marriage is unhappy, or everyone has to work too hard to keep things afloat financially, or the parents are not of a loving nature. Very often there's just not enough love to go around. Children are selfish and are constantly on red alert for what love there is. They're going to push others out of the way to get that.'

But, even if we are as loving as we can be, how – with busy lives and a million things to do each day – can we hand out even attention to each child? The answer is that sometimes we can't. Different children have different needs at different times. The trick is to ensure that children feel you are attuned to their individual needs, and that they're valued in their own right. If children think we behave differently towards them because we love them more or less than the other, then it will cause problems.

'Children will look at the amount of time you spend with them as individuals and together,' recommends psychologist Laverne Antrobus.

I advocate spending time with everybody, a fine balance I know, but if you can manage this you will set the standard and show your children you can appreciate them all.

Spending time with them individually is important and I think that parents need to be working towards spending ten minutes with each child individually at least twice a week, doing something that your child wants to do. So that means playing a game that they want or just sitting watching them playing a game. Really whatever they want to do is the key. Ultimately you are trying to give them the strong message that you value them for who they are and you appreciate the unique qualities that they have.

'I do find it hard to give everybody the same amount of attention,' reflects Mandie, who has two elder boys followed by triplets.

My eldest, Shelby, seems to think that the whole world should revolve around him. I feel sorry for Tannar, the middle child, because he's still young, but has got the triplets coming after him. But we try and make special time where we can. They take it in turns to come to the supermarket with me, which they love, because they know they'll get a treat for helping. We make it fun by having a race to see who can fill up the most bags and they'll get to sit in the front seat, which is something they all fight over.

It seems absurd, but in between going to work, doing housework, homework, school runs, making meals, sports and play dates, it can sometimes be hard to find any time at all to spend alone with children. Mothers at home complain just as much as full-time working mothers that there just aren't enough hours in the day. The best time might be after school and work but, as bedtime approaches, many parents are thinking of dinner, wine or telly rather than one-on-one time.

'Depending on the ages of your children, the ten minutes may seem difficult,' agrees Antrobus. But there is no room for excuses. 'You need to plan ahead and start small, and find times that are manageable. It's important not to get distracted, or caught up in doing jobs, or seeing to other children.'

This time is probably best achieved if you plan it in advance and let your child know when it is going to be.

Experts stress that it has to be focused on the child, rather than, for example, when making a meal, and should not involve telling him to do something, or be based around performance activities, such as homework or music practice. It could be reading a book, playing, cuddling or talking, so long as that's what the child wants to do. Meanwhile other children must be told that they are not allowed to interrupt this time; tell them that you can't talk to them until your time with their sibling is up. And take care not to talk about other children in your time alone with their sibling.

According to the theory, children will squabble a lot less if they are getting positive attention and appreciation, and will feel a lot less inclined to take out their frustrations on each other. With this in mind, I made my elder son a firm promise that I would spend some time with him one evening. The previous night he had huffed at me for ignoring him (although he had been reading in bed at the time). He immediately elected to make some fiendishly complicated science kit, which I could tell was not going to be my forte. We unsuccessfully tried to put it together for a few minutes before he patted me reassuringly. 'You're not very good at this are you?' he said. 'Let's leave it.' He sat there thoughtfully. 'But never mind. You're still the best mum in the world.' I was touched that he didn't want to hurt my feelings, and he still seemed happy, despite the failure of the kit.

Even with five children, Lisa tries to make time for all of them. 'I try to do separate things with the kids, particularly the older ones,' she says. 'I believe that it is important for them to have their own interests and hobbies without always having to have their sibling tagging along. I try to treat each child fairly by ensuring that they all have opportunities to try things they like, have space and their own time.'

Getting that individual time means hard work for Lisa every evening, starting with bottles, stories and games with the younger two children. Once the babies are in bed, at 7.30 p.m.

> *Four-year-old George and I will have a talk about*
> *our day. Then ten-year-old Henry and I will play*
> *a board game, or sometimes cards. His favourite*
> *is Monopoly but that has to be saved for an early*
> *night for the little ones and no early start the next*
> *day. Then twelve-year-old Amy is allowed to sit up*
> *with us. Sometimes we'll chat, or just watch telly.*

Not surprisingly, Lisa admits, 'I do try and reduce talking time on occasion. I do feel a bit bad, but otherwise we'd never get any time to ourselves, would we?'

I'm in no doubt that consciously setting aside time to spend with each child helps keep them more equable. But with three children it's tiring, and easy enough to let things slip. Psychologist Laverne Antrobus thinks you will quickly notice if children have not had enough attention. 'As parents we need to be alert to our children's behaviour,' she says. 'You can often spot when one of your children needs to have their special time with you, and other things need to be put on hold to allow for this to happen.'

Celebrating differences

As well as giving individual attention, the best way that we can help children feel appreciated for who they are is by fostering what it is that makes them individuals. But, according to the experts, this comes with a health warning.

While it can be fascinating to note and remark on our children's individual traits, we can easily fall into the trap of labelling or typecasting. Although focusing on an appealing trait, such as prettiness, cleverness or even being good, might be intended to be complimentary, it can become a problem for a child who might feel either that she is not noticed for anything else, or that she has to continually live up to this expectation.

'It's fine for you to notice children's traits, but you have to attend to the things that make them distinctive,' says Dr Stephen Briers.

> *You don't want to fix children into set roles by labelling them, but rather to give each one a unique place within the family by letting them know what it is of value that they bring; it could be kindness or a sense of humour, rather than whether you are captain of the football team. Your value should not necessarily be related to your performance. It's what you are, rather than what you do.*

Labelling children can make them feel pigeonholed. And while it's important to encourage children who are good at things, it shouldn't mean that others miss out, or feel that they can't match up in that area. By making statements, such as 'he's the sporty one' or 'she's the artist', it can mean that an individual child corners the market in a particular sport or subject, effectively closing it off to another child.

Charlie, who is divorced from the mother of his two sons, aged seven and eight, is concerned that they seem to have fallen into this trap. 'My ex-wife always tells the elder boy Callum that he's "the sporty one",' explains Charlie. 'Already the younger boy, Jack is beginning to steer clear of any sporting activities as he associates these with things that Callum is going to be better at. If I suggest a game of cricket or football, he shrugs me off. My fear is that he'll miss out on something that he might really enjoy, if only he'd try.' Charlie increasingly worries that Jack is struggling to stake a territory that is his own, which is having a negative effect. 'At the moment the thing he's doing best is behaving badly. I don't want "the naughty one" to become his label.'

Negative labels are also to be avoided, as a child is likely to live up to them; for example, calling a child a 'hothead' is more likely to earn you further displays of temper. However tempting it is to call your child 'lazy' for not doing his homework, or 'stupid' for forgetting his football boots, it might make him feel that you dislike him rather than the irritating behaviour. It's better to simply label the behaviour you don't like: 'It really frustrates me when you don't remember your boots.'

Nothing compares to you…

There's only one thing worse than labelling a child, and that's a comparison. Any sense that a child gets that his parent finds someone else's behaviour or achievements more admirable than his own is likely to provoke a reaction and a sense of not measuring up. Although you might feel like coming out with lines like, 'Your brother never talks to me like that', or 'Your sister's done all her homework, why can't you?' they will be guaranteed to rile.

Even when no direct comparisons are made, children can feel put down by the obvious abilities or charms of their siblings. 'It always surprises me that my twelve-year-old daughter can feel so threatened by a brother who's four years younger than her,' reflects Lauren.

> *I try to discourage them from comparing themselves in any way, but it's a minefield sometimes. I only have to praise Alex for doing something well, and Cindy sees that as a putdown. I try really hard to emphasize that they are different rather than better or worse, but they clearly still feel that they are competing.*

Clearly, outright comparisons, however tempting, are best avoided. Even if one child is better at something than another, it is best to find ways of recognising his unique abilities without referring to anyone else. Don't compare their successes to your own at their age, or even worse, tell them you were better.

'Parents have to stop themselves from falling into the trap of making comparisons,' says psychologist Laverne Antrobus. 'Sit with your partner and discuss the qualities and attributes that you recognize in your children, and then make sure you look out for anything that confirms this.'

Children's radar are also finely attuned to your approval of children outside the family; they might see your admiration as criticism of themselves, particularly if you're not strong on handing out praise. 'We always heard a lot about other people's children,' remembers Charlie of his own childhood. 'There was an extremely strong climate of approval or disapproval for what they did or didn't do. But what I always inferred from it was that if they wanted me to be more like someone else, then they didn't like the person that I was.'

Experts recommend that you pay attention to the things your children are good at, not just by telling them, but also through your actions. That means watching the school play, or sports match, even if you're not interested in football or drama, and encouraging them to try new things that will stimulate creativity and build confidence. Children who know that they are recognized for their unique abilities are happier to recognize their brothers' and sisters' abilities as well. Those who feel that they're 'not good at anything' will be more likely to undermine their siblings' pleasure in the things they do well.

'Every so often have a family review of recent achievements,' recommends Laverne Antrobus.

> *If you set this up as a known family activity you will begin to hear your children recognizing each other's achievements and praising each other. When this is reciprocated, it leads to more appreciation of each other. Children will look for the aspects of each other's behaviour that they think parents admire, or find difficult. Hopefully they will rise to the occasion and try to emulate the good bits.*

Twins, in particular, can suffer from feeling compared and labelled, and might have difficulty carving out an individual space for themselves. Claire finds this particularly hard to manage, as one of her twins, Jessica, was born with a hole in her heart and cerebral palsy. Academically she's two years behind her brother James, although her mother describes her as being 'ten years in front at getting her own way'. The children attend the same school, but they are in separate classes. 'I have to do their homework separately,' says Claire. 'It's hard for her because James will shout, "That's easy, that's easy!" at everything she does. I don't think he's trying to put her down, but he's always looking for the recognition.'

Children can also be conscious of the physical differences between them, and feel judged. My sister had to deal with constant comparisons between herself and her three elder siblings, as she looked different from us. We elder three children were fair; she was dark. Where we were lean, she was of a heavier build. 'I didn't feel part of the family,' she says now. 'You three all looked similar and I felt physically removed.'

But I also struggled in being the elder sibling to a younger brother who was small, blonde and textbook cute. I can vividly remember standing by feeling enormous, as my parents' friends cooed over him. Research suggests that my discomfort wasn't unfounded. One study found that attractive children are more likely to get preferential treatment, while another found that attractive seven-year-olds are more likely to get the benefit of the doubt after they have been naughty. Luckily, in my brother's case, it was usually me being naughty with him, so that evened things out a bit.

IT'S NOT FAIR

If a child reminds you of someone else – your irritating mother-in-law, for example – it also might have an impact on him. A child can pick up on these comparisons and not always find them favourable. 'You're like my dad. He was a great cook' is one thing. But if he knows you don't much care for Uncle Kevin, then saying 'You're so like Uncle Kevin,' is going to lead a child to his own conclusions.

Parents also need to be sure that comparisons aren't being made outside the family. Trish got a call from the school to ask if she and her husband were having problems, as their younger son, Tom, had 'shut down'. 'I took him on a picnic and tried to find out what was wrong,' remembers Trish. 'It suddenly came out that he couldn't bear to be in the same school as his elder brother, who was extremely bright. He told me, "They do nothing but compare me to Alex". Tom was feeling as if nothing he did was going to be good enough, so his way out of that was to do nothing – literally.' Trish realized that the only solution was to separate the brothers by sending them to different schools.

CHAPTER FOUR

Stop fighting

So it's time for the nitty-gritty. You've done everything possible to foster good relationships. You do your best not to show favouritism, to compare or label. You take each child's position in the family into account. You give them one-on-one attention when you can and recognize each child for their individual endeavours. But still they fight.

Do everyone's children fight? It seems that most do, at least some of the time. A quick poll of parents I know elicited the most common response: 'They'll play happily for hours and then suddenly they're killing each other.' One study found that 93 per cent of seven-year-olds fight with their siblings, and 23 per cent of those do it often.

But just because siblings are competitive and squabble with each other doesn't necessarily mean they don't like each other. In fact it's because they know each other so well that they *can* fight. Friends can steer clear of you if you wind them up too much; your siblings are stuck with you no matter what you do. 'How can you be fighting one minute and then telling each other that you love each other?' I asked my daughter at bedtime one night, as she said an affectionate goodnight to her brother. She looked surprised. 'That's what brothers and sisters are meant to do isn't it?' she exclaimed. And so it is.

While their fighting can drive you up the wall, children who never fought at all would be an eerie prospect.

Nor is fighting an entirely bad thing. Since life is such a competitive business, a bit of sibling conflict helps children test out their space in the world. Children who learn to deal with conflict at home will have had more practice at asserting themselves and will have a better chance of coping with disagreements and tensions in the outside world.

But if your children's fighting is relentless or grinding you down, then you probably need to make some changes. And since there is no magic wand to stop your children fighting, that will mean some creative problem-solving. 'You need to be pretty flexible in trying things out,' says clinical psychologist Dr Stephen Briers. 'Children of different ages and different temperaments are going to need different approaches. You need to take a look at what's happening and come up with the strategies best suited to your own children.'

Why children fight

Children fight for a whole range of reasons: it might be a simple battle of wills, a need for love and attention or the desire to dominate someone else. But different fights will mean different things at different times and you will need to respond accordingly. So it's worth thinking about some of the reasons why your children might be fighting.

Attention

'I now realize why we fought so much,' says Nick. Now adult, Nick and his brother Jimmy feuded throughout their childhood and on into adult life. They fell out so badly that a property their grandfather left them to share had to be sold and the money divided. 'It's taken me years to realize that we did it for our father's attention,' says Nick, 'because our father tried to keep our mother all to himself. He told us he never wanted kids, that it was our mother's idea. His mother had died young and he just didn't know how to share our mother with us.'

Nick's experience might be more dramatic than some, but there's no doubting that one of the main reasons why children fight is for parental attention. Broadly, if you pay attention to fighting, you get more of it, because children soon figure out that it works; but, if you don't pay children any attention when they're *not* fighting, peace might not prevail. Vanessa confesses that, like many mothers, she leaves her sons aged five and eight to get on with it if they are playing nicely. 'I just get on with chores, grateful of the peace,' she admits. 'Then someone throws a brick at someone else's head and a terrible fight breaks out, shouting, tears, the lot. And in I go.'

A child who feels that he is not getting enough attention might take extreme measures against a sibling who seems to be getting in the way. Psychotherapist Julie Lynn-Evans sees children whose fighting has become severe:

I see kids who are hitting their siblings very hard or pushing them down the stairs, or doing sneaky things like tearing up their homework. They just hate their younger siblings and are on constant guard that the parents don't spend a second more with the younger one than them. They can spend hours proving the point that the younger child is preferred. The second child then learns to fight back in sneaky ways, and will start a fight to get the older child told off. Then that feeds the system: 'You always tell me off, not her,' and so on. But by the time they come to see me it's got to the point where nothing seems to work anymore.

I often find that if I try to spend time with one child after I have been out all day, the others will pick fights to try to divert attention to themselves. The end of a working day can be a flashpoint; your children might be excited to see you, but underlying this, they might feel some anxiety about getting attention. So if you come home and think you can read your newspaper or look at mail, think again.

Something else is going on

If one child, in particular, is picking fights, she might be signalling either that she needs more attention, or that something is going on outside home that needs your help. It's always worth trying to find out more about what might be going on behind the scenes that could be triggering disputes.

Dr Stephen Briers suggests that you will need time alone with your child, if you suspect that something is affecting the way she is acting at home. But you also need to 'protect the victim and stress to the aggressor that he needs to find other ways to handle difficult feelings than beating up on a brother or sister,' he says. Equally, if you start giving a lot of attention to the child with problems, he warns that 'you need to be careful that pummeling little brother or sister doesn't become an automatic pass to your undivided attention. Keep an eye on what is being reinforced.'

Are you encouraging fighting?

Kids imitate their parents. If you are yelling and screaming at them, they are more likely to yell and scream at each other, especially if you are screeching at them to stop fighting. How often have you heard a child parroting you with expressions like, 'Will you stop that this instant!' I was quite ashamed when I heard my four-year-old say to his brother. 'I've had enough of this behaviour!' when he was still too young to know what the word 'behaviour' meant.

Children need help developing the kind of self-control most of us exert in adult life. If you are smacking your kids, it is going to be harder for them to understand why they are not supposed to smack each other, particularly when they are small and can get frustrated by their lack of vocabulary to express complex emotions. 'There is good evidence that physically punishing children is correlated with them being more aggressive over time,' observes developmental psychologist Professor Judy Dunn. 'So don't hit them. It's important that children don't learn to use aggression as a way of solving problems.'

Fighting is fun

Children can learn a huge amount through fighting: if you hurt someone, make him angry or reduce him to tears, then there are some good pointers on the impact your behaviour can have on other people. There are also lessons to be learnt from the things that provoke fights, like hitting or stealing. And sometimes having a fight is something to do: boredom can be as good a reason as any for picking on someone else.

My older brother admits that he much enjoyed orchestrating fights between me and my younger brother.

'It was very gladiatorial,' he says with relish. 'Slaps and scratches on one side, punches on the other.' I can remember getting intensely annoyed as punches always hurt a lot more, but that was the whole point. The crosser I got, the more fun it was for him.

Children are constantly testing and pushing at boundaries: it's fun to flick this tea towel at my brother, but, whoops, then it goes in his eye. It's fun to hide his most coveted football card and then see what happens when he notices it (and deny it, of course) or eat his biscuit when he gets up to answer the doorbell. It's fun to repeat the same word or phrase over and over again when it seems to provoke an interesting reaction in someone else. Some of this constant sparring can be prevented by keeping children occupied, or by reminding them that they need to get on with what they're supposed to be doing.

Do I get involved or not?

It is easy to get muddled about how to approach your children's fighting. You start out trying to ignore it, then become irritated and quickly switch from ignoring to telling off, and back to ignoring again. You walk out of the room, but the fight follows you. Then you really lose it and screech at everyone.

One study found that while many parents use 'not intervening' as their strategy, they actually do not believe that it is the most effective way of dealing with conflict, suggesting that parents are often at a loss to know what to do. Although the received wisdom may be that, if you pay attention to fights, you are only going to fuel them, you're still going to want a certain standard of behaviour in your house. This will mean acting on certain behaviour if you want to avoid it. For example, if children are hitting each other, they will need to be separated and given a clear message that hitting will not be tolerated.

The things that don't work are responses such as, 'Stop that! Pack it in!' or, 'Why can't you two stop fighting?' If you start shouting, you are probably going to raise the heat of the argument. Statements that label or compare are also unhelpful: 'Why can't you get on like so and so?' or, 'You two are always fighting', simply suggest that they can't get on and won't be stopping. Saying things such as, 'You're giving me a headache', are also likely to provoke further irritation. It doesn't help to ask who started it, or who's to blame; that simply gives one child permission to continue being aggravating.

At a certain level, the best course is one of minimum intervention, wherever possible. If you get drawn into your children's fights, take sides and dry tears, you are likely to make it all the more attractive to them and reinforce the behaviour you don't want. Even by telling them to stop, you are paying attention. Children will best learn to work through their differences if they are left on their own, provided that their verbal skills are good enough. Younger children might need your help in learning how to negotiate.

However, you are going to need to intervene if one child is being physically or verbally abused by the other (which to my mind means most fights.) You might want to try and prevent a verbal argument from escalating into a punching match. I will also act on fighting that I witness, because it's often affecting my quality of life.

Children have a right to argue, but I have a right to peace, so I can tell them to argue somewhere else. Some people advocate having a 'squabbling room', and asking: 'Where do you need to go?' whenever a fight breaks out. I haven't found this works too well, because the children's refusal to budge can cause more conflict; and, in any case, how do you do it in the middle of a meal, in a hurry getting ready for school, or on an aeroplane?

'There are no firm answers and anyone who says they've got the perfect recipe has got it wrong,' says Julie Lynn-Evans.

> *Life is life and sometimes you'll let it pass, sometimes it will annoy you more than others. But the main thing is to be above a lot of it.*

> *If you fuel it by giving it attention they'll know that they can drag you off the phone or away from your book when they want to and they'll do it more. Some days it's going to be more grating than others, a rainy day in the kitchen is far worse than a sunny day in the garden, or if you have PMT or a hangover. But the key things are not listening to the tell-tale and not stepping in unless you've seen it.*

But, she stresses, there are very clear distinctions between the everyday rough-and-tumble of children testing out their boundaries, and more unpleasant behaviour:

> *It's not rough-and-tumble if they lock someone out of the bedroom shutting their fingers in the door, or push them in the face...Children get very excitable and if someone hits their sibling over*

*the head with a badminton racket in the heat of
the moment because they're losing, that's normal,
although they need to be taught not to lash out.*

*But when it's premeditated, then it's a problem.
Tripping your sibling up so she falls down stairs, or
hiding her things so she can't get ready for school
on time and gets shouted at. That's the stuff you
need to act upon.*

Who started it? Tale-telling and taking sides

My mother's standard response to any complaint was, 'Don't
tell tales'. But to a child it's not so much a tale as an urgent
problem. 'He's just really hurt me and you don't even care!'
shouted my daughter the last time I said this to her. So,
if a child comes to you needing your help, you need to
take notice but make it clear that it won't work as a way
of getting someone else into trouble. If it is a verbal row,
you can say you are interested in how the child feels but
not in what someone else did. But, if someone is hurt or
something is broken, you will need to check it out.

Recognizing that a child needs your help is not the
same as taking sides. Even if you feel that the child who is
complaining to you has justification, it's better not to take
sides, as you never know the whole story. He might have hit
his sister over the head with a toy, but she might have been
provoking him. Don't take sides if you didn't see the fight.

If you reward the tale-teller with your anger at his
sibling, he will learn that tale-telling has a pay-off. You will
discourage tale-telling by making it clear that you expect

each child only to be responsible for his own behaviour. 'I'd rather not hear about what your brother is doing, but I'm happy to hear what's going on with you.'

'Don't get involved if one child keeps coming to you and saying that the other child is annoying her,' says Julie Lynn-Evans. 'But if he keeps upsetting her take her out for a small treat like a hot chocolate on her own, if you can, and perhaps that will send a message.'

It's also best not to pay attention if a child comes to tell you that another child is doing something she shouldn't be; it's important not to let them start trying to assume authority. Having said that, I very much enjoyed telling my parents when my brother stuck a pencil into our new space hopper and punctured it, and I enjoyed the telling-off he got too.

Don't jump to conclusions

Parents often fall into the trap of assuming that the elder child is picking on the younger. In fact little children learn very quickly that, while they might not have the verbal or physical strength, they can wind up their older siblings and then go for help when they get thumped. The younger can also be the one to start the hitting, well aware that her older sibling knows she isn't supposed to hit her. Often the one who's shouting loudest is actually the guilty (or guiltier) party. But, if there is one child constantly going after the others or picking fights, then you might need to investigate further.

'I was always sure it was my elder daughter Amy who caused the fights,' says Tom. 'But then I was watching from behind my paper one day when I saw her younger sister, Ella, purposely mess up Amy's game. Amy gave her a small push and Ella immediately turned shrieking to me. I could see how devious she was being. It really shook up my thinking.'

Set limits

Every family needs clear rules around behaviour and it's up to you to decide what you will and won't tolerate. Most families will want no hitting, biting or scratching; you may also want to include no name-calling and a rule to treat each other with respect. It also helps to establish clear rules around property and space; for example, no one is allowed to enter the other's rooms without permission. Children need to know where you stand, so hold a family meeting and tell them what the rules are going to be.

'You need a policy of zero tolerance on violence,' says Julie Lynn-Evans.

Have very clear rules on hitting, shoving, scratching, biting, and say to your children 'If I see you do it I will separate you and you will both go to your rooms or to the naughty step or have no chocolate after lunch,' or whatever works for you. You decide what the sanction is: it should be whatever works for your family, whether it's 'have your computer or TV taken away' for a time, or maybe 'you don't go on that planned sleepover'. Whatever it is, the sanction needs to be immediate and swift. But still stay as uninvolved as possible, until you have to step in.

'You have got to find a sanction that works for the kids,' agrees clinical psychologist Dr Stephen Briers.

> *If older children have established grown-up privileges, such as later bedtimes or more pocket money, then these can be taken away if they act like babies. Having to go to bed at the same time as your little brother can be a great leveller. But whatever it is, you've got to find something that hits hard for your individual child. Little ones will tend to copy big ones, so if you can stop the older ones from this kind of behaviour the problem will become less.*

Work out your strategy: what kind of fight is it?

We use the term 'fighting' as a blanket term, but children fight in a variety of ways, from petty bickering to knocking seven bells out of each other. Things with my children often move very fast: one minute my daughter is chanting a silly name at my son and he's laughing and they're tearing around; the next it's tipped over into something he doesn't like and he's shouting at her to stop, or pulling her hair. Before long someone is crying and lashing out in fury.

It helps to try and break down the different triggers to fights to work out which you can do something about, which they can just get on with, and when you want to bring in your sanctions.

He called me a...

Much of family life can be based on banter, but this can quickly tip into trading insults. No one knows better what gets under your skin than your siblings and that's why they are often so good at winding each other up. 'When barbs were hurled, you learnt to hurl them back rather than be offended,' says Anthony, one of seven children. 'But of course inside one often was offended.'

'My teenage years with my sister were spent with her constantly saying how fat I was and talking about my tree-trunk legs', recalls Jacquie, while Lauren describes how her two-year-old 'can reduce her six-year-old sister to tears by calling her a stinky poo'. In my own family my brother, who hated cheese and eggs, would be taunted with the name 'Cheggles', while our sister, who hated her bonny red cheeks, was 'Cherrychops'. Teasing was part of our family culture, and if you couldn't take a joke, well, you should chill out more. But what seems like good light-hearted fun can also be hurtful, and making this part of family culture is a bad idea.

The language that we use can have a huge impact on the emotional tone of family life. Name-calling, swearing at each other, casual insults – even if done jokily or affectionately – can all send powerful signals about what is acceptable and how members of the family see each other. Even casual remarks can trigger insecurity and affect confidence, particularly remarks about physical appearance as adolescence approaches. Since words become the chief weapon during the teenage years, it's worth discouraging name-calling from the start.

'I was listening to a psychiatrist at a conference who said, "Sticks and stones may break your bones but words

may damn near kill you" and I really have come to believe
that this is true,' says educational psychologist Laverne
Antrobus.

> *There are an awful lot of children who really
> struggle in schools or at home with being picked on
> through name-calling.*

> *Expressions of negative feelings about each other
> are all part and parcel of finding a way to live
> together. You cannot stop children from saying
> things about each other, but you can set out your
> expectations and say that it makes you upset to
> hear them talking to each other in this way.*

I marvel at the ingenuity, pettiness and, sometimes,
downright cruelty of the things my children say to each
other. This morning my daughter called my son, who's
a skinny seven-year-old, 'a fat woman'. 'Loser' is a firm
favourite with my four-year-old, though he has no idea
what it means. My daughter spent most of one afternoon in
tears because her brother kept calling her a 'lesbian'; and,
despite my insistence that this wasn't even an insult, he just
kept on pushing that button. 'Pigface, butt breath, fat slob,
weirdo...', need I go on?

    Some of this can be a testing ground for the things
you would never say anywhere else. 'It would be hard to
single out any item of verbal abuse from the torrents that
flowed in a house with four boys at different stages of
adolescence,' says Frank, of life with his three brothers. 'But
in a funny way I think verbal abuse becomes a measure of
intimacy. The things we said to each other could only have

been said between people intimate with each other. If we'd said them to friends or others, we would have been locked up.'

We might not be able to make siblings best friends, but we can encourage them to at least treat each other with some respect. I have tried a few different approaches. My elder son recently took part in a school assembly on bullying. The centrepiece of the performance was the slogan 'Think!'. Each letter stood for a question you had to ask yourself before saying something to others:

> *T:* Is it true?
>
> *H:* Is it helpful?
>
> *I:* Is it inspiring? [*My children didn't know what this word meant.*]
>
> *N:* Is it necessary?
>
> *K:* Is it kind?

I've found it very effective when one child automatically calls another 'fat pig' to ask them, 'Did you THINK before you said that?' Then they all chant, 'Is it true, is it helpful, etc.', which, if nothing else, can help break the moment of tension and distract them from thinking up more names for each other.

I also told my children that I would dock 1p off their pocket money for every nasty thing I heard them say to someone else; and if they came and told me about each other, they would both get docked. The trouble was that the four-year-old is still too young to really appreciate the benefits of pocket money, so he spent his entire time hurling insults and then suggesting, 'Mum, you should dock them'. The other children would also argue about who should get money off, and whose fault it was. This approach seemed to breed more resentment.

'To stamp out name-calling you have to deal with it like a significant issue,' says Dr Stephen Briers. 'Have a conversation with your children and say, "It is not OK to call people names. I don't want you to and, if you do, you will go to bed early tonight", or whatever other sanction you have decided on.'

But what happens when a child comes to you saying her brother has just called her a name, or alleges he said it under his breath so you didn't hear? 'As with all crimes you have to have the hard evidence,' says Dr Briers.

> *You have to have witnessed it. But if a child comes to you and says he called me **** you can say, 'That's horrible, stay away from him.' You can go to the other child and say 'Your brother says this, you need to know that if I hear that, there will be trouble.' Sometimes the child will admit it. If you've witnessed it, or got a confession, you can go in hard. And if it goes on they will both get a sanction they don't like.*

'You can also have a star chart for the person who doesn't name-call,' says Julie Lynn-Evans.

> *When you get a certain number of stars, you get 10p or a visit to buy football cards, or whatever has currency for the children. You need to sit them down very quietly to explain. If you name-call, you will lose computer time, or whatever your sanction*

is, but if you don't you will get a reward. And the only judges are Mum and Dad, and never ever waver!

He's annoying me – squabbling

The constant sniping that goes on in our house is probably the most wearing aspect of parenting for me. It starts at 7 a.m. and can go on unabated until the children leave each other at the school gates; then it starts up again as soon as they arrive home. The other morning I heard my four-year-old shout, 'Loser!' from his bedroom before he had even got out of bed.

But this isn't so much about name-calling as constant low-level bickering. Watching my children I can see that there is often someone playing the role of provoker, for no apparent reason; this might involve doing something irritating, like repeating everything someone else says or singing the same song or saying the same phrase over and over and over again. The more one child reacts, the more the other will say it:

'Don't do that.'

'Don't do that yourself.'

'Stop copying me!'

[*Mimics.*] 'Stop copying me.'

'Shut up!'

'Mum, he told me to shut up. Shut up yourself!'

This sort of bickering seems to occur mostly when children

are bored, tired or hungry. Sometimes it's obvious what is causing their frustration, but often it appears to be entirely random needling to get a rise. For example, when I handed my two sons a sweet each, they started squabbling:

> *ES:* [*Gesturing towards his brother's sweet, which is the same as his own.*] That's a baby sweet. And everyone who's a baby eats it. You're one.
>
> *YS:* I'm not one!
>
> *ES:* You are.
>
> *YS:* Mum! He's telling me that I'm a baby.
>
> *ES:* Because he's eaten the baby sweet.
>
> *But later he's conciliatory.*
>
> *ES:* You can have the first rice cake because you're the biggest.
>
> *YS:* But you said I was a baby.
>
> *ES:* I know. I was only joking.

A classic trigger for bickering is the desire to divert attention away from the child who's getting it. My son was trying to teach me the words of his concert performance, but his sister was going to make sure that the enterprise had to be aborted by making constant niggling interruptions, accusing him of kicking her seat and claiming that everyone else was annoying *her*. Often children will blame each other for anything that ails. 'I'm late down this morning because she turned off my alarm clock'; 'It's his fault I'm grumpy'; 'I have to bang the ketchup bottle on the table because *he* finished it,' and so on.

'James knows he can wind Jessica up and he knows that will wind me up,' says Claire of her eight-year-old twins.

I take one of two approaches: either I walk off into another room, or I join in. The educated part of me says, 'Calm down,' and the other part ends up screaming at them. I'm forever shouting, 'Stop fighting!' Then sometimes I'm in the kitchen and I hear them start up and you get to the point where you think, 'For God's sake!' and go storming in.

Like Claire, I try my best to grit my teeth and ignore a lot of this. But when I'm upstairs, trying to get ready to take the children to school, and I can hear the child who is being goaded shrieking with increasing volume, it can be absolutely maddening. I don't always manage to stay calm.

'You've got to remember that squabbling children are getting something out of it,' says Dr Stephen Briers. 'In some way it's emotionally gratifying for everybody, even if they are hurling abuse. So the most effective thing is to stop the interaction and split them up.'

Dr Briers recognizes that:

You can't always necessarily deal with it there and then. If you can't send everybody into separate rooms, you can impose a two-minute silence. It's pleasant conversation or no conversation. But later you will need to revisit this and tell them: 'If this goes on you will have early bed, or you won't watch your favourite programme', or whatever other sanction you have in mind.

Dr Briers is clear that, once you have set limits for your family, you can use your rules to nip this kind of annoying behaviour in the bud:

> *With older children once you have explicit rules it means you can penalize stuff that seems minor. The rule 'we treat each other with respect' means that even if you're doing something minor like whistling under your breath, it's no different to the physical stuff. If he's whistling under his breath he knows what he's doing. Once you've identified it as a problem, then it's a zero tolerance approach.*

Even something like whistling is worth heading off at the wind-up stage, as so often a fight will escalate from there. 'I wind my brother up,' admits Jack aged eight. 'Then he gets so annoyed that he starts hitting me. We fight, then I punch him in the face and he cries to Mum.' If Mum is going to have to step in at some stage, better sooner than later.

I put this strategy to the test. My middle son likes to tap his feet and hum under his breath. His elder sister hates it, so it's guaranteed to get her going. The tapping and whistling began. I told him that it was likely to provoke other people and that he should stop it now. He carried on, so I reminded him that early bed was the sanction for people who couldn't respect other people in the house. He stopped. It worked! Since then I have been much tougher in stamping out wind-up type behaviour. Rather than ignoring it, I'm now intervening much more quickly to try and divert conflict before it escalates.

It also helps to try and motivate children not to bicker, particularly at mealtimes, by praising them for good behaviour. You might be able to head off an explosion, especially if one child does not rise to the bait: 'Even though your brother was teasing you, you have not said anything back. Well done'; or, 'You're sitting next to each other nicely and no one is squabbling.'

Some experts encourage a mediation type approach, where you can intervene in order to help children sort it out for themselves. This works best when there is a clear point of dispute: you listen to each side, without apportioning blame and state each child's point of view; express faith in their ability to work it out, make a suggestion if you need to and leave them to it. I put this to the test when a row seemed to be building in the garden. 'You want to play with the ball, but you want the space to be clear, so you can do running,' I reflected to my bickering daughter and son. 'See if you can find a solution. Why don't you make a new game with running and catching in it?' and I shut the garden door. Instead the screaming just got louder, so five minutes later the children were all ordered inside.

He hurt me – dealing with aggression

We have a no-hitting rule in our family, which includes pushing, biting, kicking, pinching and hair pulling. But unfortunately that doesn't stop it from happening. My four-year-old, in particular, is going through a brutal phase. One minute he's hugging his brother, the next his brother is crying and there's a bleeding scratch on his back. 'Well he deserved it, he was teasing me!' says the little cutie.

'It actually isn't relevant who started it,' says clinical psychologist Dr Stephen Briers. 'Regardless of how you were provoked it isn't OK to thump someone. If you've hit someone you've allowed yourself to get drawn into it.' Dr Briers suggests that you do two things:

> *One, you stop the fight there and then; two, you can address the feelings and consequences later.*
>
> *If children are hurting each other or about to hurt each other they need to be physically separated. Send them to separate rooms to cool off. You might not be clear who touched each other first, in which case the sanction applies to both.*

If you have sanctions in place for fighting, then these should be used.

'I've got a big whiteboard in the kitchen for their bans,' says Mandie, whose two elder sons fight frequently. 'If they hurt each other, they get banned from using the computer or watching the telly. Shelby has lost time on the computer, so he can't talk with his friends on MSN, or he has his PlayStation taken away. He can hit hard and I don't think you can let that go.'

The rule of thumb remains that, if you didn't see what happened, you can't act upon it, unless there is a visible injury. My daughter came to me saying that her youngest brother had pinched her. I didn't really respond, but later noticed red weals on her back. 'What are those marks?' I asked her. 'I told you,' she said angrily. 'He pinched me – and you said nothing!'

'In a case like that you need to apologize to the child and explain that because you didn't see it happen you couldn't act,' says Dr Briers. 'But now you have seen the marks you will need to go and find the other child and say 'I have noticed, I'm not pleased and next time I will be angry.'

If you have witnessed one child hurting another and it's clear who the aggressor is, then you can also deprive the aggressor of attention by focusing on the victim. This way the victim feels safe while the aggressor gets no reward for her behaviour. Later on when tempers have eased, you can talk calmly to each child about what happened and how best it might be prevented from happening again.

But it's important not to lose your temper, or react to fighting with aggression yourself. If you become angry when your children are fighting, you might lose control. One mother reported that her husband got so frustrated he knocked the children's heads together. This is not to be recommended. While it can be tempting to say, 'I'll show you how much that hurts!' and inflict it on the perpetrator, this would be sending out a very mixed message.

Lisa was furious with her husband, Ian, when he encouraged ten-year-old Henry to hit back at his elder sister in front of their younger children:

> We were in the car when Amy and Henry's sniping
> at each other advanced to attacking. What started
> as a simple game of spot the Mini Coopers soon
> turned into each accusing the other of cheating.
> Amy hit Henry and he was reduced to tears, so
> Ian told him to hit her back. But it never stops
> there, so the two of them were actually fighting in
> the back seat. I ended up shouting at all three of
> them, Ian included. His argument was that it was
> a taste of her own medicine, but how can you tell

*the younger ones that hitting is wrong if Daddy
is actually telling Henry to do it? I don't believe
smacking is the answer to any problem.*

Children who witness physical violence in the home or on
TV are more likely to imitate it. Jay, who had witnessed
his mother Kathy being beaten up, started acting out what
he had seen, using his little brother as victim. The way in
which her sons were fighting terrified his mother. 'Jay gave
Owen a black eye,' Kathy recalls. 'He got hold of Owen's
head and rammed it into a wall in front of us. They would
pick up stuff and hit each other with it. I didn't like to see
it happening and was very worried that one of them would
get hurt.'

Kathy was able to recognize that Jay was acting out
the violence he had witnessed as a young child, and that
she had to learn to be alert to the warning signs of a fight
so she could step in before the violence started. To begin
with she and her new partner had to watch Jay playing with
his younger brother, and be very firm if he was aggressive.
'For a while we couldn't let them be alone together at all,'
says Kathy. 'I liked to keep them in my sight when they were
playing and even now I'll just keep an eye out. If they're
upstairs, I'll pop my head around the door to check what
they're up to.'

Often physical fighting is an expression of anger and
frustration, so the more you can do to help communication
the better. You can teach children safe ways of expressing
anger and frustration, such as thumping pillows or kicking
a ball. Physical exercise can also be a great way of diffusing
aggression, so if the fur is flying, get everybody out.

Motivate kids not to fight

When Lesley decided to take her nine- and ten-year-old sons, Ben and Sam, to a psychologist, to try and resolve their fighting, the boys sat down on the sofa and started kicking each other. 'She immediately gave them a star chart and said "Right, you two are *not to touch each other* for a week,"' says Lesley. 'It changed my life in an instant.'

For each day the boys got through without touching, they received computer time or collectible cards. Lesley recalls that the change was instantaneous:

> *Before I couldn't pull them apart, and their fighting was really vicious. I realized that every morning I had been thinking 'I wonder if I can have a shower, or get dressed before they fight.' That immediately went. After three or four weeks of the chart they had broken the cycle. I had been spending far too much time sorting things out, trying to be far too psychological with them. Now if they start I just say: 'No, into separate rooms' – it's brought me back into control.*

As with any area of discipline, reward and praise for good behaviour works better than criticism and punishment for bad. Notice, as much as possible, when children are getting along nicely, and say so.

'If you have a no-hitting policy, with penalties for hitting, it's important that you also incentivise children,' agrees Julie Lynn-Evans.

> *So that if you don't hit for a week, you get a pound, or a trip to the park or a DVD, or whatever works*

as the best currency. Each individual family has to find its own rewards as well as sanctions. Older children want to be recognized as older, so if you behave you get an extra half-hour at bedtime or another privilege, which singles you out as the elder child. The message is there's something in it for you if you behave yourself.

Kathy used a sticker chart and reward system to motivate seven-year-old Jay and five-year-old Owen, who had been fighting very aggressively. For each part of the day that they didn't fight they got a sticker, and a marble, which they put into a jar and were able to exchange for treats. If they fought, they got a black cross on the chart, and no marble. She also talked to Jay about fighting and encouraged him to come and tell her when he was feeling cross. 'I found the sticker charts helpful for quite a while,' says Kathy, 'right up until the point where I felt I didn't really have to use them any more. It wasn't so much the stickers or even the rewards that the boys cared about; they hated getting the black crosses and would compare with each other. So then they'd try and work harder at it.'

Kathy also tried to reduce aggression with more physical affection for her sons. Jay's violence had made her stand slightly apart from him when in fact what he needed was physical reassurance. 'They still fight of course,' she says. 'But what's changed is that when we stopped being so stressed by it and took a calmer approach, he learned to calm down too. The aggression went away when we started to recognize it.'

They're being mean to me!

Many of children's games can include an element of boundary pushing, which might mean inflicting pain on others. These seem to divide broadly into the experimental:

> *My brother asked me to put my finger near the hinge of a deck-chair to see what happened. I made him swear he wasn't going to close it, but he did, very hard. The nail came off soon after...but I think he was experimenting rather than being cruel.*

> *I shot my brother at point blank range on the forehead with a gun that fires suckers. It hit him so hard he fell over and had mild concussion.*

> *I once made my younger brother stand against a post while I attempted to throw a tent pole with a spike into the fence above his head. I threw as hard as I could and it scratched a groove in the top of his head and then stuck firmly under the skin. He bled everywhere. And he still has the scar today.*

> *I was cooking chocolate brownies and my brother was nagging for a spoonful of mixture. So I gave him a spoonful of catfood instead as it looked dark and brownie-ish. I'll never forget his face.*

And the downright nasty:

> *She locked me in a shed and went in for tea and forgot about me. That's why I'm so terrified of spiders now – the whole place was crawling with them.*

THEY STARTED IT!

The Typewriter game meant sitting on the younger sibling's stomach with your knees on his hands to stop his arms moving. Then you 'typed' on his chest, throwing in an occasional bell 'ting' with a swift strike to the face.

We used to climb onto the top shelf of the wardrobe in my sister's room by balancing all the board games and pillows in a pile and climbing to the top. It took my little sister ages to get up there and, when she did, my older sister and I would jump down, take down all the board games and pillows, shut the wardrobe doors and leave her to cry until my mum found her.

I once stole one of my brothers' sparklers. They retaliated by setting my hair on fire, then cut it and sprayed it with hairspray. I was told to tell Mum I'd been playing hairdressers with the dolls.

There are also many wind-ups, which take the form of pranks. 'I needed to leave my plate of egg and chips on the table to go to the pantry and so I counted my chips to make sure none were stolen in my absence,' recalls Frank. 'I came back to the table and only after satisfying myself that all the chips were still there noticed that the egg had gone. After much hunting, I found it on the floor under the sofa.'

Blurring the borders between fantasy and reality seems to be a recurring theme, particularly where there are younger children with less sophisticated powers of reasoning. Nicky, aged thirteen, told her eight-year-old sister that their parents were looking for a place for her in the children's home. Steph took a similar approach with her younger sister Margaret. 'I put a lot of time and effort into telling my sister she was adopted,' she says. Grace, whose sisters were nearly eight and ten years younger than her, told them that they were both adopted, and that their real parents were coming to get them. 'They were really traumatized,' Grace now remembers. 'The younger one was terrified every time the doorbell rang. She thought it was social services coming to get her.'

I was quite good at the imaginary wind-ups myself. I used to play pretend games with my little sister but sometimes allowed the boundary between fantasy and cruelty to blur a little. In one game she was going to boarding school (aged three). I packed a tiny toy case for her, and persuaded her that she was really going to catch the train to take her away to school. Needless to say she was terrified.

When is it bullying?

While there's no such thing as 'harmless' teasing, some unpleasantness between children can slip into the realm of being deliberately cruel. My younger brother recently confessed to remembering that he used to get the cigarette lighter in our car (when such things still existed) and threaten to brand our younger sister with its red-hot tip. Although it never actually happened, this could be loosely described as mental torture.

'My brothers had a particularly unpleasant game where they would have fun either teasing me or scaring me until I was blubbing my heart out,' recalls Julie, whose two brothers were six and nine years older than her. 'Then they would take a photo of me crying. We actually have photographic evidence, which still makes my blood boil. I used to moan to my parents about it, but the general response was just "Keep out of their way and they'll leave you alone."' Because her parents didn't intervene, Julie learned to put up with their bullying. 'I just trailed along behind them and stopped complaining. I think I felt that my brothers were entitled to be horrible to me. That's what brothers do, right? But they pushed it too far at times.'

'Bully' is an emotive word, and not a label to stick lightly on your child. 'For behaviour to be seen as bullying it needs to be repetitive and entrenched,' observes psychotherapist Julie Lynn-Evans. 'All children can be cruel and naughty. Most children can be educated, bribed or punished out of cruel behaviour. However, when cruelty serves the child in that he gets attention – even if it's negative – or feels more like the "top dog", bullying will set in.'

Because our sister was seven years younger than me and five years younger than my other brother, we sometimes found her gullibility overwhelmingly tempting. My younger brother used to enjoy pretending that there was a fire under her bed (he could do a very good imitation of crackling flames) or hiding in her cupboard to jump out at her. He even persuaded her once that her duvet had come alive and was going to consume her. We used to wait until she had ascended the stairs and then turn off the lights using the downstairs switch so she was plunged into terrified darkness.

Was this harmless fun? My mother would accuse me of spite, which was never an emotion I recognized. I don't remember feeling any malice towards my sister – in fact rather the opposite. But, if it amused us, then it was certainly cruel at times. Luckily Julie Lynn-Evans agrees that this is within the realms of normal behaviour. 'Poor child,' she observes, 'it's funny, but it's not spite or malice. A younger sibling can often become a toy; parents need to protect the younger ones and educate other children.' My sister is less certain. 'The laughter is what makes you feel so excluded,' she reflects. 'It might be fashionable to call it bullying now, but I did feel very unloved at times.' I hope that I've made it up to her since.

If you keep accusing one of your children of bullying another, then there's a chance that they will turn it into a self-fulfilling prophecy, by falling into the roles of bully and victim. If a child believes he is a bully, he will act like one. Instead of calling him a bully help him see that he can be kind, and help siblings see him in a different light by saying positive things about him.

As in the case of Jay and Owen, who were imitating the viciousness of adult fighting, parents need to watch out if they notice that one child is more aggressive than another. If you suspect one of your children of bullying another out of your sight, it's worth having a chat with both sides on their own, and trying to find out whether they are angry or sad. 'Bullying is probably an unconscious desire to make oneself feel better by bringing someone else down,' says Julie Lynn-Evans. 'By definition the bully is unhappy within herself and missing something, or she would not be needing a leg up at the expense of another.' A chance to talk about how she feels and to suggest ways of improving things can help break a pattern of behaviour.

If a child is feeling victimized, it could help to suggest how he can stand up for himself next time it happens. Don't always give comfort to the victim or you will encourage him to play this role, especially if he's getting someone else into trouble at the same time as getting sympathy. It's worth breaking the cycle because child bullies can grow up to be adult ones, while those who are bullied can have problems with relationships and self-esteem.

Cut down your fight quota

It's usually possible to work out the flashpoint times in your family. Children mostly fight when they are bored, tired or hungry, or any time when you're in a hurry and they can feel your stress. Breakfast time is always a red-hot zone in our house, especially before any food has gone down. If you can identify these times, you might be able to change your strategy. For example, if the children are tired, let them watch TV; or if they are restless, let them play a physical game.

If your children are fighting more than usual, it's also worth asking whether they are getting enough sleep. 'I think my kids' fighting all depends on how much sleep they've had,' says Mandie. 'And then how I deal with it depends on how much sleep I've had. A lot of it is the weather too. Once they can get outside and we can go to the park after school, everything is a lot easier.'

Many mothers agree that regular exercise and being outside the house can have a hugely improving effect on children's relationships; the playground, soft play areas, swimming or walks are all possible escapes for tetchy siblings. It might also help to encourage different hobbies at home so that, even when in the house, children can spend some time away from each other, but occupied.

Friends coming to play can also be a flashpoint. 'If one of them has a friend, it's a nightmare,' says Lesley of her sons Ben and Sam. 'Sam's friends wind up Ben. Ben's friends don't want to play Sam's rough games. It's always a potential tinderbox.' Some of my children's worst fights have been when I have got a friend each for my older two children. Instead of each one being content with their friend, it has turned into a 'boys *v* girls' standoff, with accusation and counter-accusation of teasing and 'spying' on each other.

Because children have to learn to exercise far more self-restraint around friends than they do with each other, the mix of siblings and friends can be explosive. It is worth laying down some ground rules before friends come round; I no longer allow more than one child to have a friend at the same time as it provokes too much fighting.

Preventing fights outside the house

If you're going on a trip, especially in the car, it's worth setting out rules before you go, and praising children for doing well along the way. If you offer bribes for behaving well, then these should be received after the journey, rather than when you set off. For example, if you say, 'I'll give you a comic each for no fighting in the car,' it needs to be bought as soon as you arrive. If you buy it at the start of the trip, then it's not going to be linked to the behaviour and the chances are you'll get fighting *en route* while the comics don't get read.

As for my children attacking each other in the middle of that busy beach (see pp 1–2) what could I have done?

I decided to separate my sons and made them sit separately off the beach with my husband and I. Dr Briers thinks I could have gone further:

> *By the time they are all fighting, the only thing you can do is march them all off to the car to think about what they're doing. They all need to sit there for 15 minutes – you probably only need to do it once.*
>
> *The problem is as a parent you want things to be nice. But if you want to stop it happening again it's probably worth the investment to make the principle. Later on you can talk to your son about his justifiable feelings of anger at his castle being smashed down. It will reinforce what matters if you show you haven't forgotten.*

Mandie reached the end of her tether when her two boys, aged nine and eleven, started punching each other in the middle of a crowded restaurant on holiday:

> *Everyone was walking around them, trying to get to the food with these two slugging each other. Eventually I just screamed: 'Will you all just stop right here!' and the whole place went quiet. Then this woman asked if I needed any help. 'Not unless you work for social services and can take the kids away,' I replied. She meant did I need help carrying my tray! Anyway it helped end the fight.*

Practise conflict resolution

Professor Judy Dunn, who has studied sibling relationships over long periods noticed 'intriguing results' when observing quarrels:

> We watched how mothers dealt with conflict between themselves and their children when they were little. Then we looked at how the children sorted out their own quarrels with their siblings when they were older. With the mothers who took the child's point of view into account and encouraged compromise or negotiation, we saw this reflected in the way the siblings sorted themselves out later on. There's no doubt that the use of talk – learning to appreciate someone else's point of view – is very important.

So, if there has been a screaming match, it helps to get both sides together and find out what happened without laying any blame. Each side should be able to have their say without interruptions. Acknowledge feelings rather than get stuck on what happened. Then recap so that everyone agrees what each side said. Ask each person to say what *they* could have done differently. Ask them to say, without blame, how they would like the other person to behave in future. You can write this down, or write down an agreement with all parties agreeing how to behave in future. Respecting your children's point of view in this way will help them feel listened to.

Because children will be aware of how you resolve conflicts as a parent, it always helps to say sorry. I am prone to the odd outburst (known to my family as 'shout-ups') and, because I know it's a less than desirable way to behave, I always make a point of apologizing quickly to anyone caught in the blast. I think that, if you apologize for moments when your own behaviour is less than ideal, the children will learn to follow your example. I've noticed now that my daughter is much quicker to apologize if she knows she is in the wrong.

Although forcing a child to apologize means that she might say it without meaning it, it helps children to learn that apologizing usually means the end of the dispute. It is useful for children to acknowledge that they might have hurt someone; sometimes they might come up with other ways of making amends, such as making a card, or drawing a picture.

Break that habit

It's worth remembering that children fight because it's fun, and that as a habit it can be hard to break. It might even take twenty years, as Anthony's experience as one of seven siblings bears out:

> *I remember one Christmas when I was in my early twenties. It was like every Christmas I could remember, in that there was a loud, hurtful fight going on in the kitchen amongst several of us. Usually one snaps at another, and a third joins in with their pet view, which triggers the involvement of another and so on. On this day, Mum just started crying and shouted, 'WHY must you always fight with each other? Why can't you get along?'*

She was so upset, thinking that her children just didn't like each other. We all tried to comfort her in various ways, laughing and saying, 'We just fight because we always have. It doesn't mean anything,' because it never did. We never stewed, and apologies were rarely offered or required. We just got over it. On this day, amongst the washing-up of the Christmas lunch, we told Mum that we wouldn't fight anymore like this, because we didn't want her to be upset. And somehow we managed to be true to our word. In the years that followed we began treating each other more as individuals rather than as scratching posts.

So don't give up hope!

CHAPTER FIVE

That's mine

My house often resonates with cries of 'Giiiiivve iiiiiiiit!' 'That's mine' and 'Give it back!' Children are naturally territorial and will wrangle over ownership of anything: a seat, a toy, a place in the car. If someone else has got it, they want it. Only the other morning my daughter sat at breakfast with a football tucked under one arm rather than allow her younger brother to use it.

When I was growing up, my parents used a set of tablemats for place settings. Each mat had a different colourful picture of a bird on it. My brothers, sister and I decided that a particularly brightly coloured and lively looking bird was 'the best bird' and so the fight commenced to get that mat at every meal. Whoever set the table naturally would award themselves the best bird, but that didn't mean it would stay there. By the time the meal began, the best bird would have been switched around several times over, with corresponding levels of squabbling and outcry: 'I've got the best bird!', 'That's not fair, it's my turn!' The mat could even be switched as the plates were cleared before pudding, or if you were foolish enough to leave the room in the middle of the meal.

Various rotas were tried and failed until in desperation our parents bought another set of identical mats. Now there were two best birds, only the new set of mats had the names of the birds on, so we immediately declared that the new best bird 'didn't count' and went back to our warring ways. This went on until we were well into our teens. The moral of the story? Well, children will fight over anything, but sometimes trying to make it right for everyone just doesn't work.

Encouraging sharing

Travelling recently on a packed London Underground train, my three children had to share two seats. The whole carriage looked on in amusement as my four-year-old stood there yelling, 'That's *my* seat!' at his elder brother, who was nudging his sister insisting, 'Move!' She, in turn, argued, '*He* took *my* seat, I'm not moving!' They displayed none of the customary self-consciousness of the Tube traveller; I was aware of everyone watching with interest to see how I would resolve the standoff. Eventually I had to grab the four-year-old and hoist him, protesting loudly, onto my knee. It struck me that this scene was a great example of how uncooperative siblings can be with each other at times, and how unwilling they can be to come up with effective compromises.

Wherever possible, we try to encourage sharing by setting examples. We have a bit of a mantra in our family, which is: 'We're a family, so we share'. It doesn't always work, but it's gratifying to hear the children saying it to each other, admittedly in a rather aggressive way at times, when someone wants a bite of someone else's cake. When they do share, they get lots of praise.

What doesn't work so well is when we try to force it on them. My three children were each given a present by relatives; the boys got two small things each but my daughter got seven small things (I don't know quite what the givers were thinking). Needless to say there was an immediate outcry and the general reflection that it 'wasn't fair'. The boys demanded that their sister 'share' some of her present. I could see that she was struggling with this, but beyond endorsing that it would indeed be nice if she did feel like sharing something, I didn't make any demands of her. After all, it was her present. Eventually she took one of the smaller packets of felt tip pens she'd got, and divided it between the two boys. 'Big deal!' grumbled my elder son, but I thought she deserved praise for recognising that she had got more than them, and for taking a small step to rectify it.

Seven presents versus two seems pretty uneven; however, it is a bad idea to try and prevent sharing wars by buying the same of everything. Children don't need duplicate toys, although everyone will want their own major items, such as bikes. What works better is to point out the advantages of sharing to children: 'You've got a scooter, and you've got a skateboard, so you can both get a go on a different thing and have more fun that way...'; or, 'You've got six computer games each, so if you share that makes twelve'.

'Sometimes putting the children in charge of sharing can work,' says Susan who has four children. 'If I say to them, "There's only one biscuit, what's the best way of sharing it?" they can actually be quite cooperative with each other.'

While my children can be remarkably stubborn about sharing, there are also times when I can be moved by their desire to divide things between themselves. So long as they are in control, they can be extremely benevolent. My four-year-old recently managed to resist eating the last three chocolate buttons in a packet on his way back from a party, because he wanted to give one each to his brother, sister and father. I found his self-restraint touching and admirable, especially as I was trying to talk him into giving those buttons to me!

Promote sharing from the start

It's important that children get used to sharing with their siblings from a very young age. Once a new baby becomes mobile, the whole dynamic between her and her older siblings will change. Now she no longer has to sit and wait for them to offer her toys to look at: she can get them herself. This is inevitably a rude awakening for an older child, who might have no desire to share graciously.

Sharing needs to be encouraged with a great deal of praise; simply insisting that an older child shares his toys as a matter of course is likely to breed resentment. It might help to distract the older child while the baby crawls about, or to quickly offer something else to the baby, who might not yet be so fixated on particular items that she notices. You can teach the older child to do this too. But don't immediately expect the older child to be keen on sharing, particularly if the baby is sucking and drooling on things.

One strategy that works well is to set up a special area or shelf for the older child, where he can keep toys, which the baby can't yet reach. But if the older child becomes aggressive, he needs to be firmly reminded that hitting isn't allowed. He can learn that it's OK for him to say 'No' firmly, and then gently take the toy back; and if he can be encouraged to offer the baby a substitute toy, all the better.

'Ruby used to go really wild when Elinor started messing up her stuff,' remembers Anna. 'I found it really helped to appeal to her sense of being more grown-up. I used to say things like 'That's so kind of you to help me with the baby. I know it can be annoying, but you're such a big grown-up girl.' I think it really boosted her confidence, and helped her be more caring about her sister.'

If this strategy falls flat, then a star chart can help motivate a child aged three or over, with small treats, or special time together as a reward for good sharing. This helps reinforce the behaviour you want, although it needs to be kept up consistently to be effective.

Turn-taking

Learning to take turns is important. As well as being encouraged to share, children can learn to take turns from quite a young age. Waiting for a turn on swings is a good example: children have to wait for their turn, and then get off, usually before they want to, to give another child a go.

If children can't share something, then taking turns can work as an alternative. When both my sons want to sit at the tap end of the bath, I set the kitchen timer and give them five minutes each. But that doesn't mean turn-taking always goes smoothly. My elder son recently came back from a party and offered a toy lizard he had been given to his younger brother to 'share'. Inevitably they then could not agree on whose turn it was to have the lizard. 'Well it's mine really,' declared my older son. 'So I should decide on how long I have it for.' 'But you said you were going to share it,' I pointed out. 'Yes I am,' he said. 'But it's my go now and I want a long one!' Eventually the shouting and yelling about the lizard reached such a peak that I decided that no amount of turn-taking was going to work. So it was removed and placed up on a high shelf until they could sort themselves out. I noticed the other day that it's still there, entirely forgotten.

Personal property

Just because children are siblings doesn't mean that they have to automatically share everything that comes into the house. Every child has a right to some personal property, and it helps if you have a clear idea of what you think it is fair to expect them to share. While objects like TV and computers (in main spaces) are clearly communal, if children have personal possessions or favourite toys, they should be allowed to keep them to themselves, and have some choice over how and if they want to share these.

In my family, Bearby, my daughter's well-worn teddy bear, is clearly off-limits and everyone in the family knows that they would not play with Bearby, unless they were specifically invited to do so. The other day I overheard my younger son saying to his sister, with the inimitable logic of a four-year-old, 'Right, that's it, I'm killing Bearby!' – the ultimate threat.

If children want to protect personal property, they need to learn to keep it in a special place, such as a shelf or drawer, or in their bedrooms, where it will not be in the way of other children. You can make a rule that things in the child's personal space are not for sharing without the child's permission but that, if things are left out, they can be shared. If fights break out over items, they can be confiscated.

'How do we stop the little ones messing up stuff?' asks Lisa, who has five children.

Well, first rule is, if you don't want it touched, put it away! If it's been left lying around and not moved after warnings from us, then I'm afraid we have no sympathy. On the whole this works reasonably well. The older ones keep precious stuff in their rooms. Henry (ten) has some special cars that he keeps separate, and trading cards the others know not to touch. Amy (twelve) keeps her stuff in her room. It's too far up at the top of the house for anyone to bother going up looking for mischief.

Children should have the right to say who is allowed to use their things. But you might need to help them negotiate what happens, and think of appropriate consequences, when things are borrowed without permission. If something gets broken, for example, the borrower might have to replace it from pocket money, or lend something of hers as a substitute. The other day my son lost a week's pocket money for ripping up a CD cover belonging to his sister; this was his way of expressing his dislike of her music, but he needed to learn that damaging someone else's property is not acceptable.

Arguments over communal items like TV or video can be simpler: if they can't agree, then off it goes. Computers cannot be reserved for personal use, except at pre-agreed times. Some parents also report that some of the computer or PlayStation games that need two players offer an excellent way of uniting children who can't share against a common enemy.

'The things that everyone has trouble sharing are the TV and the computer,' agrees Lisa.

> *We try to alleviate this by allowing each child an allotted time limit, such as twenty minutes on the computer, or one whole programme. Then it's the next child's turn to choose what to watch. This works quite well when I'm around to supervise. But if I'm distracted, then invariably the bigger ones will try to take advantage, which always ends up with them shouting at each other.*

Sharing bedrooms

Not all children can have the benefit of their own room; sharing a bedroom can be both intimate and fun, and lots of siblings enjoy it. For children who don't get on, however, it can highlight the differences between them. 'I had to share a bedroom with my younger brother for too many years,' says Patrick. 'Now I hardly see him. We spent so many years being pushed together. Perhaps we said everything there was to say to each other.'

For younger children there can be benefits in sharing a room – creating extra time to play together and helping them to share. 'I think it stops them from getting too territorial about what is "theirs",' says Kate, who has always put her three children, now aged eight, six and three, in the same room, despite having enough space for their own rooms. Her main reason for doing so is her memories of the constant 'Get out of my room!' arguments between her and her three siblings when they were growing up. 'It means they share their toys more freely and sometimes it's quite cosy for them. But I don't know if I will go on doing it for much longer,' she admits. 'The older ones are beginning to ask when they can have their own rooms.'

Even if children are sharing a bedroom, it helps if each child has some personal space, which they can call their own, or a specific spot where they can put things, which the other kids won't interfere with. Sometimes a curtain or partition can be made to provide some privacy.

When Vanessa's family had to move to a smaller house, her two sons had to go from having their own rooms to sharing with each other. 'Archie found it hard to go from having his own space to having to share with his little brother,' says Vanessa. 'He started getting very stressed about it, so we built him a sort of tent-like bunk space over the top bunk, which he could retreat into. He finds Charlie very annoying at times and it helps to have a refuge from him.'

Creating a private space in the bedroom can also work well where younger and older children have to share a room, but have different bedtimes. It is not realistic to expect the older child to have lights out at the younger child's bedtime, but if she has a space where she can perhaps read with a small light, or sit up a bit longer, it helps emphasize her more privileged status as the older child.

Property wars: when to step in

Sitting on a holiday beach, I noticed two little sisters playing together. They were happily splashing around with buckets and spades, until they decided to build a sand castle. Both picked up the same watering can at the same time and neither wanted to let it go. A tug of war ensued, punctuated by loud screams. What interested me was that their mother appeared to be looking right through them. She sat staring in their direction, watching the fight, but doing nothing. Eventually the larger child wrestled the can from her sister's hand and the small one slumped to the ground in tears, still appealing to her mother for help.

The starting-point for this kind of fight is often actually *before* the argument breaks out. If you take the time to notice and point out when children are playing and sharing nicely, they will be less likely to suddenly spark a fight to get your attention when something goes wrong. Although the girls' wrangle over the can didn't get much attention from their mother, she also seemed oblivious to her daughters when they were playing so well.

But once a sharing dispute is underway, knowing when to step in and when to leave children to it is key. If someone is getting hurt, or they are unable to reach a satisfactory agreement, then they might need your help. Leaving one side lying sobbing on the sand doesn't seem like a satisfactory conclusion.

One way of intervening before things get out of hand is to ask children who owns the item over which they're fighting. If someone owns it, then he should be allowed to choose whether he lends his property or not. Rather than suggesting that he should give up something he doesn't want to, it might help if you ask him to suggest something he *would* be happy to lend. Children love to perceive themselves as generous; letting a child know that he is being helpful and giving him lots of praise for his kindness can boost his sense of benevolence. Alternatively, you can try and help the left out child find something else to play with, which might help break the fixation on one particular object. In the case of the watering can, which was probably a family item, the mother may well have been able to suggest that the girls take turns, or distract the younger child with something else.

If two children are arguing about something that is easily divided, then it's possible to suggest that one does the dividing and the other chooses which bit he gets. This approach works for pieces of cake or Lego but, if there are more than two children, it can become rather complicated and you might have to do the dividing.

But what's most important is that you don't take sides. By ordering one child to give something to the other, you are leaving children in no doubt as to who is the winner and who is the loser, which will leave them feeling that you are showing preferential treatment for one over the other.

Mediating sharing wars

Some experts think that the best tactic, when children are having a sharing dispute, is to intervene briefly and then leave them to sort it out for themselves. If you take this approach, you should step in briefly to find out what each child's point of view is, and state the case back to each in turn, saying to one child, for example: 'You want to play with the toy garage'; then to the other, 'Your garage is special to you and you don't want it to get broken'. Then you should state what might work best, or the rule, if there is one, but leave the children to decide whether to negotiate. For example: 'It's your garage and your decision, but if you want to work something out with your sister that's up to you'. Then you should leave them to it.

That's the theory, at least. I put this one to the test on a Friday afternoon. Everyone was fairly tired and my younger son had a friend to play. My daughter had been briefed to leave them to it. Then everyone came hurtling into the kitchen, the argument already at full throttle. The boys had elected to play a Nintendo game, but my daughter would not let them play with the game they had selected, which belonged to her. She claimed that, last time she lent it to her brother, he 'messed it up'. He vehemently denied this and was already in such a rage that he was screaming, 'She's lying!' at the top of his voice. There followed all sorts of intricate details from my daughter about the alleged crime, punctuated with louder and louder screams from her brother.

I asked my son to calm down and try to say what he wanted without screaming. 'You want to borrow the game,' I said to him. I turned to his sister, 'But you're worried that it might get broken'; then speaking to both, I suggested: 'If games get broken, then they can't be lent.' 'But,' I told my daughter, 'it's your game and your decision. Perhaps you can do a trade with your brother.' At this point I was meant to withdraw but things moved too fast.

'OK,' she conceded, and my son grabbed the game before the deal had been struck. 'I want Frank Lampard!' (a much prized football card) she demanded. 'No way!' he returned. 'OK, your computer time [one hour, allowed at the end of the week]', she replied. 'NO WAY!' he shouted. I wasn't supposed to be intervening at this point, but tried to steer them back on track. 'What would be a fair trade?' I asked. 'My homework!' said my son, who had already started playing the Nintendo game and was looking cocky. 'Yeah how about a piece of old paper,' joked his friend. This wasn't going to work. My daughter was furious. 'I want my fair trade!' she shouted at me. 'Why haven't you sorted this out?' Eventually she ended up snatching the game back, with my son screaming at the top of his voice again and the friend standing, looking as if he would like to melt into the floorboards.

If children are unable to settle disputes on their own, a next step might be to call a family meeting to agree a solution. So this is what I tried the following day. Each child got the chance to give their point of view without being interrupted, and only after that could there be any rebuttals. Then we wrote down a list of possible solutions, with everyone contributing and no judgement being passed, to see if we could find one on which we all agreed. Inevitably the row about breaking things started up again, as well as the argument about my son's unwillingness to trade fairly. But my son's point of view got to the heart of the problem: 'I let her borrow any of my Nintendo games she wants,' he complained. 'But when I want to borrow hers, she always says, "No, they're special".' 'Well, they are special!' reasoned my daughter.

The solutions we came up with were quite varied: 'Don't let anyone borrow anything,' was one of them. But eventually my daughter agreed that she would nominate one or two 'very special' games, which would be for her use only; aside from these, she agreed that she would share her games with her brother as much as he did with her. In this way, they would both get the use of as many games as possible. But, if there was any evidence of his 'messing up' the games again (which he still hotly denied), then all lending would be revoked. Both children seemed happy with this agreement. And I'm pleased to report that it seems to have worked. There haven't been any significant game wars since.

CHAPTER SIX

Testing times

All families have their ups and downs, but there are some situations that may affect children's behaviour and the way in which they deal with their siblings. Children are creatures of habit, and often find it hard to cope with change; they may also take it personally or blame themselves for things that are beyond their control. Disruptions, such as illness or death in the family, marriage breakdown, difficulties at school, or problems with a sick or disabled sibling, can make it hard for children to cope.

A sudden increase in sibling conflict may be a sign that all is not well in other areas of their lives, or that they are struggling to cope with a change at home. When my husband suddenly had to spend a lot of time away for work, my own children displayed a sharp increase in sibling fighting. Perhaps they felt that they needed to grab my attention to ensure that I didn't go away too.

A child who suddenly displays a lot of anger at his siblings may actually be angry about something entirely different. 'You may find that children "act out" when there are times of difficulty,' says psychologist Laverne Antrobus. 'Often their behaviour reflects the worries they have and their need to communicate this in some way. Children may become withdrawn or behave badly to distract their parents from the issues that are causing distress.'

When a family breaks up

With up to one in four marriages ending in divorce, and many other unmarried couples with children splitting up, the reality of family break-up is something that a lot of children face. It can be a sad and confusing time for them. Children may feel in some way responsible for what has happened, and end up shouldering a heavy burden; if they play up or test you by fighting more with siblings, it can be a sign that they need your support.

For Claire, a period of severe health problems coincided with the collapse of her marriage, which meant a very stressful time for her then seven-year-old twins James and Jessica. Jessica had been born with health problems, and James took the new situation to heart. 'He started playing the man-of-the-house role, disciplining Jessica and telling her to go to her room,' says Claire. 'I didn't know what to do with him. Eventually I asked a teacher to have a chat with him and he told her, "My mum's poorly and my sister's poorly, so I have to sort it out." It was heartbreaking. I felt like we'd taken his childhood. He needed reminding that he was still a little boy.'

Stuart, now thirty-eight, only realized as an adult why he picked on his younger sister so much. 'My parents' marriage took years to go down the tube and there was constant friction between them,' he recalls. 'The tension in our house was dreadful. But nothing was ever clearly articulated. I think I was acting out my own fear at what was happening. Also there was so much shouting and yelling going on, it seemed only natural to push how I felt about that onto someone else.'

'The main rule about marital conflict,' says clinical psychologist Dr Stephen Briers, 'is not to enact it in front of your children if you can possibly help it. Otherwise, children may feel they have to take sides, or end up "siding" with different parents and this can then alienate them from each other.'

Despite your differences, it's important to present a united front and not use the children to complain about each other. Even if you are separated, avoid using the children as a conduit for communication or asking them to choose between parents. The more children see you dealing calmly with conflict, the less likely it is to overspill into their own lives and relationships. 'Some parents tend to turn to one or more of their children for solace,' says Dr Briers. 'Making Mum or Dad feel better is not a burden that any child should have to shoulder. The resulting pressure is likely to drain a child's emotional resources and increase existing tensions in sibling relationships.'

Experts agree that if your relationship is going through problems and there are changes afoot, it is important to be as honest as possible in telling children what is happening. Although children don't need the gory details, it helps to keep them in the loop so that they understand what is going on. But don't be surprised if they do play up, or fight more with their siblings.

'Some acting out between siblings is normal and maybe inevitable,' says Dr Briers. But this doesn't mean that parents should tolerate antisocial behaviour:

> *Because they feel guilty, parents often end up accepting extreme behaviour they would never normally tolerate from their children. In reality the children, who are likely to be feeling insecure, need gentle but firm handling if they are to feel safe.*

The message is that although family arrangements may be in a state of flux you are still in control and capable of looking after them.

Children within the same family may experience divorce differently. The impact may be less severe on older children, especially if they already have some independence outside the home. Gemma found that her younger children were very open about her marriage break-up, but that the older siblings bottled it up. 'Outwardly they were very cool,' she says, 'but it was much harder to glean whether they were hurting.' If a parent has left, children may also test the remaining parent or siblings with difficult behaviour, perhaps as a way of ensuring that those left stand by them.

Marriage break-up doesn't always have a negative effect on sibling relationships; in fact, in some cases it can strengthen the bond. 'The children seem to form a solid pact when anything happens, usually them versus me,' says Jean, who is a mother of five. 'They were angrier with me when their father left, because they blamed me for him leaving.'

There was a surprise benefit for Stuart after his parents divorced: his relationship with his sister dramatically improved, partly because they now found themselves united by a new enemy. 'We bonded over our loathing of the new woman our father married,' he admits. 'From our teens through to adulthood, it's given us a lifetime of having something in common.'

Building new families

It's inevitable that after death, divorce or separation, parents are going to meet, marry, or move in with, new partners. Officially 11 per cent of families are stepfamilies; in reality this figure is probably far higher, as it doesn't include unmarried families who live together. As new families are formed, children have to cope with a number of potential changes: moving in with a new family, or visiting one regularly; getting a new parent and stepsiblings, or experiencing the birth of half-siblings.

Children who are being brought together to form a new stepfamily may feel that they have lost something: a parent, or their place in the family; if they have had to move home, they may have lost their school, friends or their own room. A child's place in the pecking order may also shift between two families; the eldest in one family may join a stepfamily with older children and quickly have to get used to being in the middle. A teenager who suddenly inherits a family with younger children may be daunted by the new prospect of hanging around with toddlers.

Building new families means a lot of work: the children will need extra attention at the same time as their parents are focusing on a new relationship. Where there are children on both sides, parents will need to make a conscious effort to spread their attention and not just concentrate on their own kids; it can be hard to manage everyone's needs and wishes. Parents have to work hard not to treat their own children differently, or show any favouritism.

'I find it's really important to give each child time alone with each parent, away from the other siblings,' says Angela, who has two stepsons, as well as two daughters of her own, one of whom was born with her new partner. 'I make as much effort as I can to spend time alone with my stepsons as if they were my own. The only problem is we have to put our own needs on the back burner sometimes, and that means little time for me and my husband to be alone together.'

'Try not to force relationships,' advises psychologist Laverne Antrobus.

> *Encourage children to share their thoughts; it is important to know what each member of the 'new' family is feeling. Do not try and convince them that everything will be fine; by removing the pressure to get along relationships may emerge in a more natural and genuine way.*

Lisa's elder son ten-year-old Henry is from an earlier relationship and has a different father to her three younger children. Henry and his younger brother George fight for attention from his dad, Ian. 'I think that Henry is a bit jealous of the fact that Ian is George's dad and lives with us,' says Lisa, 'whereas his own dad, although he sees him, doesn't have an awful lot to do with him emotionally. Henry is an emotionally needy child and needs to know that he is as important to you as you are to him. I think this is where a lot of the arguments come from.'

When stepsiblings don't get on, Antrobus suggests:

> *You will have to make it clear that the usual rules, such as respect for your authority and each other, remain essential. You and your partner will have to keep 'getting along' high on the family's agenda by providing opportunities for each child to choose a favourite meal or activity that they enjoy. The more*

*love, respect and consistency of care that children
are shown as individuals, the better they will feel
about themselves and be more likely to behave in a
generous way towards new stepsiblings.*

When two families come together, space is often at a
premium and bedrooms can be a bone of contention.
While, ideally, you may want to remake a space, rather
than shoehorning children into the existing rooms, this
isn't always possible. Where stepchildren are visiting on a
regular basis, but not actually living with the family, they
can feel pushed out by the lack of personal or private space.
It's also not uncommon for the children of the father to feel
displaced, reflects psychotherapist Julie Lynn-Evans:

> *A new stepmother tends to make the home and
> tends to keep custody of her children, so they will
> have their own bedrooms...The father's children,
> who are more likely to be living with their own
> mother, are going to have to share when they come
> to visit. There's a lot of 'there's no room in this
> world for me, I'm always second best'.*

Lynn-Evans suggests that you listen to these grievances and
take them seriously:

> *Say 'It sounds like you are getting second best, and
> you're not making a fuss.' With bedrooms children
> do need a reality check, because of course it's
> about economics. But they also need to be heard,
> that it's really tough. Then you can help them think
> about what you can do about it together.*

When parents in a new relationship then add to their family, thus introducing a half-brother or half-sister, this can also put pressure on existing children. A new baby can create a bond between children who aren't related, as they will both be related to the baby; but they may also feel hurt and rejected. Angela's stepson Eddie was thirteen when she and Eddie's father had new baby Daniella. Angela recalls:

> *He started attention seeking at school and playing up at home. He told his dad that he felt pushed out and that no one had any time for him any more. Meanwhile my daughter Alexa was delighted, and loving to the baby, which I think annoyed him more. It took a long time, and a lot of focus on my part, to rebuild the relationship with him. One thing I think helps is not using the term 'half-sister or brother'... Daniella is Eddie's sister as far as I'm concerned.*

When a child has special needs

Having one child in the family who is ill, or who has a disability, can put extra pressure on the whole family, including sibling relationships. Inevitably it shifts the family focus if one child is needier than the others. This can sometimes be a positive experience, drawing the family together, but if a sibling feels that she is somehow invisible, because of the special-needs child, it is more likely to breed resentment; she might feel jealous or angry at how much this one child is able to demand, and seek ways of getting attention. Alternatively, she might feel that whatever her problems are, they aren't as bad as her sibling's and so bottle things up.

'I saw one girl whose older sister had Asperger's Syndrome,' recalls psychotherapist Julie Lynn-Evans. 'She described her sister as having stolen her life. She'd been told thousands of times she was lucky, but all she really felt was that she was second-best.' But Lynn-Evans acknowledges that parents have to be realistic about life with a child who has greater needs than the others:

> *If you've got a child who particularly deserves one kind of attention, it makes complete sense that you are going to get sibling rivalry. A 'normal' kid will forever feel he has less time and energy from the parents and is trailing along behind. So you need to draw in wider society as much as you can, whether it's friends, teachers, godmothers, you need to do everything you can to widen your support base. Find a way, however you can, to have special time with other children. But also you have to realize that you're doing the best you can as a parent and that you've been dealt a tough hand.*

One of Mick and Claire's twins, Jessica, was born with a hole in her heart and learning difficulties. Their understandable anxiety about Jessica meant that her brother James felt that he rarely got a look in. 'He used to say to me, "I hate you, you love Jessica most", and that absolutely freezes you inside, doesn't it?' says Claire. As the twins grew up, Jessica learned to manipulate her parents' fear that she was more vulnerable to injury by adopting an untouchable stance when she and James fought.

'When they were smaller she would scratch, bite, pinch him and he used not to hit her back, because he was so worried about her health,' says Claire. 'He would get beside himself saying, "Don't hurt her don't hurt her!" if I so much as tapped her hand.' But now the twins are eight, Jessica is stronger. 'It's his payback time,' says Claire. 'Now he really lays into her.'

James alternates between protectiveness of his sister, and frustration that she is not as able as him. 'On the whole he's loving towards her, he'll help her do her shoes, because she can't do them,' says Claire.

> *Sometimes I check their rooms in the night and find them in the same bed, cuddled up. But he loves to mimic her and wind her up, too, and she really annoys him. They both have a Nintendo DS and he'll set hers up for her; but then she still finds it too complicated, so she'll start annoying him and poking him. It's a shame because he's the one, who's been sat nicely playing, and then she gets hit round the ear and he's in trouble.*

While a child may resent his sibling for getting more attention, it can't be used as an excuse for bad behaviour. Understanding the illness or disability may help reduce tension and aggression: keep siblings in the picture and let them know what's going on if there are changes afoot, or hospital visits to deal with. Make sure that siblings have someone to talk to about their fears and anxieties.

It's also important to focus on what a special-needs child can do, rather than what he can't, and to encourage his abilities wherever possible. Make it clear that no one in the family is a 'problem'. If a sibling feels that the other child has special allowances made for him, this may lead to friction.

Thirteen-year-old James had health and speech problems as a younger child, meaning that his parents, John and Nia, got into the habit of babying him. But, as he reached his teens, this began to cause problems in his relationship with his fifteen-year-old brother, Dominic, and there were frequent fights. Nia admits that James used his earlier problems to wrap her around his little finger: 'Because of his illnesses and disabilities, I've been able to mother him more than his brother,' she reflects. 'I do connect better to James than to Dominic.'

But Nia and John realized that James was using his apparent vulnerability to manipulate his parents and that, by treating him with kid gloves, they were driving a wedge between the brothers. By giving in to James and not making him face up to taking more responsibility, Nia and John were unwittingly making it harder for the boys to get along. It was also affecting James's ability to act more maturely. The brothers got along far better once Nia and John stopped making so many allowances for James.

An able-bodied sibling can also feel great pressure to succeed and achieve all the things his sibling will not be able to. 'My father adored football and was desperate for his son to continue his love of the game,' relates Douglas. 'My brother's got Down's Syndrome so I felt that I had little choice other than to become the football player.' This can become a burden. 'Actually I hated football,' says Douglas, 'but I also felt guilty about having so much more than my brother. So I felt obliged to get on with it.'

The special-needs child may also feel conscious of, and even guilty about, the effect she is having on her siblings. Sally, who is partially sighted, feels that her disability was a nuisance for her sister, Stella: 'She was younger than me, but actually felt more like my older sister because I often needed to ask her to help me,' she remembers. 'Sometimes she could be really helpful, but then at other times she'd get shirty and accuse me of treating her like a servant. I know my disability affected her life too.'

Problems outside the home

If your child is facing conflict, at school or within his peer group, you may see a change of behaviour in his dealings with siblings at home. If he seems suddenly angrier, or if there is a new and seemingly inexplicable increase in fighting, it could be a sign of difficulties beyond the immediate family. It's worth asking your child about what is happening outside the home, although he may need some encouragement to tell you the cause of the problem. Is he really angry with his siblings, or is his anger a sign that something else is going on?

'The best thing you can do with an angry child is listen,' advises psychologist Laverne Antrobus. 'Even though you may not want to hear what he has to say, or agree with the source of his anger.' Listen as closely as you can to what your child might be trying to tell you. If he is reticent, you could try an opening gambit, such as, 'It seems like you're feeling bad today', or you could suggest what the problem might be: 'I know you get really upset when you don't get picked for the team. Is that what happened today?' The child will be more likely to correct you. If you can get to the root of the problem, you can help your child problem-solve. Showing that you take the problem seriously helps.

School plays a big part in a child's life and if things are going badly at school, it may affect her sense of self-worth. Similarly, if a child is being bullied she is likely to take it out on someone else. You may need to talk to teachers to see the bigger picture. Teachers can help you recognize your child's weaknesses and strengths: whether you have, for example, unrealistic expectations of what your child can achieve, or whether an unrecognized learning difficulty is causing her to take out anger and frustration on a sibling.

For Lisa's eldest child, Amy, the transition to secondary school has seen problems in her relationship with her younger brother, Henry. 'I do think that secondary school has something to do with the fact that they don't get on as they used to,' she says.

> *I can understand this, as no one wants their younger siblings hanging around when they're trying to be cool in front of new friends. I can't accept her using Henry to show off in front of her friends, however. She tends to let him join in a bit, then just tells him to get lost, this upsets him, he gets annoyed, she starts shouting louder, being lairy, and then I need to intervene.*

My seven-year-old son suddenly started being much more aggressive, and then at other times more tearful. It seemed like his siblings could get a rise out of him more easily than usual, but he would overreact so dramatically that he was starting to be an easy target. When I spoke to his teacher, she reported that nothing was wrong in the classroom, but after more probing, she discovered that he was being left out of games in the playground by two of his friends. This was leaving him feeling vulnerable and anxious, which was causing the trouble at home.

Although my son was reluctant to discuss what was going on between him and his friends, just acknowledging that he had been having problems and showing that I understood, seemed to help. I organized for each of the friends to come and play, in turn, and as so often happens with children's upsets, the dynamic between them shifted and everything settled down again.

CHAPTER SEVEN

Getting along famously

I love the way moods and expressions flitter so briefly across the face of a sleeping baby. It seems to me that children's relationships are like this: constantly shifting, nebulous, often changing mood or direction before you can even get a handle on what's happening.

Sibling relationships are like many other facets of family life: they have good days and bad days. Sure, my children fight, but it would be a huge simplification of their relationship to say that's all they do. They can move seamlessly from an argument to playing marvellous games together and at times are extraordinarily loving and kind towards each other. There are times when I look at them and think, why can't they always be like this?

It's touching to see my daughter sitting down to help her brother with his homework because she hasn't got any and she 'wants him to have more time to play'. If one of my children is genuinely crying and upset, the others will often try to comfort them. When my elder son had a meltdown over football cards, his sister made him a 'feel better package' containing some of her own cards, as well as some things to make him laugh. We can't always influence these moods, but there are some things we can do to encourage our children to get on with each other.

Equally, there are some things we have to learn to accept. Perfection is a fantasy. 'Parenting is a dance and it needs to be as elegant as possible,' says psychotherapist Julie Lynn-Evans.

> *But the steps are always changing. Your job as a grown-up is to adjust the tempo of the dance. We've got to allow for being creatures of our moods. Although we want consistency, it's a dream. We have different moods and so do they. But, if you stick to the basics, like no hitting, and make sure that you show equality of love and that everyone is as important as each other, you'll be pretty much OK.*

Top tips to help your children get on

Having spent the last few months taking a candid look at children's rivalry and fighting, I have drawn up a checklist of top tips that you can practise to help your children get on – while also ensuring that you make that parenting dance as smooth as possible.

Accept what you can't change

If you're beating yourself up about your children's inability to get on, don't. Sibling studies suggest that children's personalities have a large impact on how they get on; although you can have an important role managing conflict, it's not your fault if your children irritate each other. Some sibling relationships are simply going to be harder from the outset and that's the way it is.

Whether children are easy-going or have more challenging temperaments will have an impact on how adaptable they are, and how they get along with others. Just as children show marked differences in the way they react to the birth of a sibling, those who are more emotionally explosive can find it harder to share, and are inclined to react more intensely to disagreements. Research has found that, if children are temperamentally mismatched, there's a greater chance that there will be more quarrels.

Lesley's two sons, Ben and Sam, are only fifteen months apart but it wasn't until she visited a psychologist, at her wits' end with their fighting, that it was pointed out to her how different they were:

She said to me, 'You couldn't get two more different children.' Ben is emotional, a phenomenal reader, has less friends, likes learning; Sam can barely read, is sociable and sporty and likes playing. Although I knew they were different, I hadn't realized that it was that complete differentness which was creating the conflict between them.

They are so different in every way that if they weren't brothers they just wouldn't have bothered to get to know each other, their paths would never have crossed. They've got parents in common and live in the same house, and that's about it. I realized they don't have to love each other, just cohabit congenially. That came as a revelation to me.

Promote good communication

The family culture in which children live is going to be a strong influence on how they behave towards each other. Children will learn from example, so, if you use a lot of teasing or sarcasm, don't be surprised to see it reflected in their relationships. I grew up in a very noisy shouty family, and it's easy to see the same traits emerging in my own family. If the tempo in your house is fast and furious, it helps to try and turn down the heat.

'I'm not a dog!' said one mother in response to her kids' continually yelling out her name. I've also got very fed up with people yelling out my name, wherever I am in the house, so have instituted a new rule that, if anyone wants to talk to me, they have to come and speak to me in the room where I am. I'm trying to follow the same rule myself, although reminding three different people in different parts of the house that they need to put on their shoes and clean their teeth *now* – and without raising my voice – can sometimes be a challenge.

It's also helpful to try and frame things in a positive way, rather than barking out constant commands. 'Please could you put your plate in the dishwasher...' is going to go down better than, 'You've left your dirty plate on the table *again!*'

It's equally important to listen, and to create opportunities for children to talk to you and tell you things. We sometimes go around the table at mealtimes and offer everyone the chance to say what was good and bad about their day, which gives children a forum to be heard. Discourage children from interrupting each other, and don't interrupt yourself. Let everyone have their say. The car and bath-time can both be good for one-on-one moments of focus.

Some children are excellent at garnering your attention no matter what you're doing. My four-year-old just says, 'Mum!' repeatedly, whether I'm working, on the phone or have my head in the washing machine. But other children can be more reticent and, if I don't make time to talk to them, or look for quiet moments when nothing else is going on, they might not be heard.

Face up to feelings

Family life can be incredibly intense and children's feelings towards each other can be a rollercoaster, ricocheting between love, hate, anger, indifference, jealousy and warmth. They can fall in and out with each other with remarkable speed

Children often need help in identifying their feelings, and families that encourage listening and are open in talking about feelings will find it easier. Children will sometimes need help learning how to handle frustration and anger; how we respond to these feelings will help them appreciate how other people feel, too, and the impact they can have on other people's feelings.

It can be helpful to practise 'reflective listening' (see p 61), where you acknowledge what the child is feeling by reflecting it back, or tentatively acknowledge the feelings behind what the child is saying. You might suggest, 'It seems like you're upset,' or, 'I wonder if that makes you sad?' This can be a useful tool when children are expressing negative emotions.

Our instinct when children say things like, 'I hate her!' or 'I wish he was dead!' is to tell them that they mustn't talk like that, or to say: 'No you don't, you love her.' Rather than bat it away, try to listen and help the child identify what she is feeling by putting those feelings into words. Instead of trying to take the feelings away, it's a way of offering support and showing that you understand. 'It feels like you hate him at the moment because he broke your game. That makes you feel bad.' Listening reflectively means understanding why the child is saying these things, by stating how you imagine she must feel. You can also take a guess at what the child might wish could happen: 'You wish he would treat your things carefully,' and suggest ways in which the child can express her hostile feelings without hurting anyone, such as by drawing a picture.

The first time I tried it, I was quite taken aback by the response. 'You feel annoyed that your sister knocked down your tower,' I said soothingly to my infuriated son. 'Yeah I really hate her for that,' was the response that fired back. 'I guess it can be frustrating sometimes when your work gets broken,' I suggested. 'Yeah I'd like to squash her head with this brick!'

'If you use this technique you have to be prepared to follow it right through,' says clinical psychologist Dr Stephen Briers.

> *No matter what the child says he wants to do, you can't shy away from it. The point about naming the feelings is that once they're named they can seem more manageable. Putting it into words can actually have a containing effect.*

I tried again with my son. He got into a white-hot rage with his sister because he felt so frustrated at being left out of her game with their younger brother. Having screamed at her he retired simmering to his room. 'It makes you angry when they leave you out,' I suggested. 'Yes it does!' he replied angrily. 'You wish that they would let you join in?' I asked. 'Yes' he hissed. 'You know if you feel angry you could draw an angry picture or write it down,' I tried. 'Then I'd just be angry, angry, angry *all* the time,' he spat. 'I've been angry with her my whole life!'

We sat in silence for a few minutes, and then his anger just seemed to slide away. 'Hey Mum,' he said after a while. 'Do everybody's hearts beat at the same speed?' And the anger was gone.

I have to praise you

It might seem obvious, but children respond far better to praise than they do to criticism. It can help boost their confidence and motivate them to earn more praise. The more positive attention you're paying children, the less inclined they will be to play up; and if they feel positive about themselves, it might help them feel more upbeat about siblings.

Often when children get things right, or do what we ask, we don't even notice. It's very easy to fall into a pattern of pointing out what they're doing wrong, and getting annoyed when they ignore you. If a child has been causing you grief, it can be hard to notice things to praise. So however small the things are that they are doing right, tell them. 'They all shine at something, whether it's drawing, table manners, behaviour,' says Mandie of her five children. 'If one of them has been helpful or well behaved, then they get lots of praise. Praise, praise, praise, that's what I try and do as much of as possible.'

Children respond much better to specific praise, rather than the more general 'good' or 'bad' type comments, or vaguely effusive praise. If you just keep saying to children, 'You're so brilliant,' without ever being really specific, then it's hard for them to know what you expect. Specific comments work better, like 'Oh you're putting your shoes on really well', or 'Thank you for hanging your coat up'. Sometimes you can simply describe what they're doing in an approving tone: 'You're writing very neatly,' or, 'You're sitting and eating so nicely'. But it shouldn't be over-egged or children will sense you are insincere.

Each child's unique contribution to the family needs to be acknowledged; it helps to notice even small acts of kindness. It's good to acknowledge when children are being nice to each other, being generous or sharing, and to praise older children for helping with the little ones. When my daughter gets her little brother dressed in the morning, I tell her, 'That's really helpful of you to get your brother dressed when you know I'm in a hurry. He is so lucky to have a kind sister like you.' The more opportunity you give children to show that they can be cooperative and helpful, the more this will help build on their sense of self-worth within the family.

'I get Tannar to sit in the bathroom with the triplets while they are having their bath,' says Mandie of her middle son. 'He helps them and I give him lots of praise for looking after them. I make a real point of saying well done to him.'

Mandie also always makes an effort to notice when her children are playing nicely:

> *The other day we came in from school and had a really nice afternoon. For once no one was fighting. I didn't get stressed making tea and they were all on the trampoline and enjoying playing together, so when Matt got home, I made a real point of saying to him that we'd had such a nice afternoon and thanking the children for being so nice to each other.*

Use rewards

Some parents baulk at the idea of having to bribe their kids to do what they want, or even worse, paying them to be nice to each other. While praise is the best reward for being cooperative, rewards, if properly used, can also help reinforce good behaviour. Clearly, if a child says, 'I'm only going to do it if you give me 50p', then it isn't working, but if children learn that behaving in a certain way gets them something that they like, then they are going to be more likely to keep behaving in that way. The other advantage of using rewards is that they can provide a useful bargaining tool: if you don't get the desired behaviour, you can withhold them.

Think about what your kids value and enjoy. In my family it's cash and play dates for the eldest two, magazines and bedtime stories for the youngest, and TV and computer for all. It's very important to think about what matters to your children because, if they don't think it's worth their while, they're not going to make the effort. Similarly, if a reward is too big or too far away, a child might not be able to keep up the motivation: 'Be nice to your brother every day this month and you can have an iPod for Christmas,' for example, might make it too hard to sustain the effort.

You can create a star chart – for not fighting, or name-calling, or for being nice to each other – with small treats given at the end of each day (ideally not food or sweets). At the end of the week these can be tallied up to make a larger treat, such as an outing or a small gift. The important thing is that the reward be given as soon after the good behaviour as possible. Equally it's very important to make sure that you follow through and give the reward you offered.

Practise negotiation skills

It sometimes seems to me that my children can never agree on what we should do as a family. One wants to go to the park, one wants to play tennis, one wants to stay at home and no one wants to compromise. Whoever gets overruled can fly into an appalling rage.

Holding family meetings can help children to learn ways of negotiating what they want and understanding that different people want different things (see pp 103, 143). Family meetings can be an excellent way of ensuring that everyone's voice is heard and can be a regular slot for a family get-together. Everyone can discuss any issues affecting family life and grievances can be aired.

Family meetings can help children to come up with solutions and encourage problem-solving, although it is important to acknowledge that, if one child doesn't get what she wants, she might feel upset about it, and those feelings should be allowed. Everyone should be given a chance to speak, with no one interrupting, which might mean sitting patiently while the four-year-old makes his point about wanting more sweets.

Help siblings look out for each other

I sometimes find one of my older children tucked up in bed with their little brother, reading him a story. It makes for a sweet scene. The praise they get for being kind to him makes them feel that they have got something to contribute to family life, and this is more likely to make them want to do it again.

Encouraging children to look out for each other can help strengthen the bond between them, although this shouldn't be confused with asking elder children to help with little ones. Caring about the feelings of brothers and sisters can help children develop empathy; understanding how others feel can help them to get along. These feelings can be apparent in times of real distress, when I have been moved by my children's attempts to comfort each other. After several days of fierce fighting, my daughter was ill in bed. Her brother came home from school and laid his head on her chest. 'I wish you could be well again,' he said. When my son appeared to be unhappy at school, my daughter told me that she was looking out for him, not because I had asked her to, but because she wanted to. He noticed too; he separately told me that she had comforted him when he had been crying in the playground after being hurt in a game.

I was really touched the first time my elder son stepped in to help his younger brother a couple of years ago. There was some argy-bargy in a playground and a bigger child pushed my youngest son over; as he swung around he came face to face with my elder son. 'Leave my brother alone,' he said fiercely. Then he reached down and picked up his little brother from the ground and tenderly brushed him down. I was heartened by a sudden vision of the two of them years hence, standing up for each other outside some pub.

Encourage play

There seems to be some truth in the old saying, 'The family that plays together stays together'. Of the many people I have talked to, it seems that those who played a lot with their siblings in childhood have stayed closer in adult life too. My younger brother and I spent hours playing imaginary games around the house, and all my siblings still speak the stupid language we made up together. We also played a lot of board games, which lead to dreadful fights, but were a useful way of learning either how to cheat or to be a good loser.

For modern children the lure of electronic games and TV can pose tough competition with playtime; I try to limit these games as I have noticed that the more time my children spend in separate activities the more disparate they seem to become. Once the electronics have been switched off, and the more time they have where nothing in particular is happening – usually at weekends – then they will drift into playing together. They can play amazingly elaborate games, involving dressing up, bits of paper, lists, charts and cards. They play shops, schools, parenting, potion making. My daughter

devises endless trading and marketing schemes.
In our tiny London garden they kick balls around,
whack them over the fence and against the kitchen
window, roar around on bikes and scooters, balance
along ledges, climb on tables. But it's still sometimes
hard for them to find a game that they all enjoy
playing; my middle son is often to be found, out
bowling a ball on his own, having tired of the
elaborate imaginary games.

While children are still little, they need your
supervision but once they are big enough to be out
of your sight, they are best left to it, unless their
play is getting rough. Research suggests that make-
believe and fantasy games help children develop
social interaction skills and learn how to interpret
other people's thoughts and feelings.

While parents don't want to interfere in imaginative
play, there are ways you can encourage children
who don't play together much to do more together.
Simple card games, such as Snap or Uno, can be an
excellent start, even with quite young children, and
it's good to think up activities, such as helping in
the kitchen or the garden, where everyone can take
on a role – each one as important as the other – to
achieve an end result.

Limit rough play

Sometimes it can be hard to distinguish between
my children's play fighting and actual fighting, and
the boundaries between the two are fluid. One
moment my two boys are jumping on my bed and

giggling, and then they're suddenly in a bundle, red-faced and kicking each other. I step in and separate then, reminding them that there's no kicking in our house, and even before I've turned to walk away the giggling and jumping have started again. I don't know if families with boys are more prone to this kind of behaviour, but watching my children scrap, roll, giggle and tweak does remind me very much of puppies.

'Stop rough-housing!' was my mother's refrain for years. Looking back, it sometimes seems as if we spent our entire time jumping on each other's backs, rolling on the floor and shrieking. Understandably, it drove our mother mad. I don't particularly subscribe to the 'it didn't do me any harm' school of thought; I can't say now what the benefits were of having had someone force my arms up behind my back, or pin my legs behind my head, and then sit on them. But perhaps all that rough play did help make me more resilient.

Expert opinion generally seems to be that rough play is alright, so long as it doesn't go too far, and so long as there is not a huge imbalance in strength or age, which can make it harmful. It helps teach children what their limits are, how great their strength is and can even help them control aggression. But you will need to keep an eye out and call a stop to it if it is getting out of hand. It should also be discouraged as children move towards adolescence and become much stronger, particularly if they are different genders and likely to become unevenly matched.

When it isn't working

Although we all want our kids to be the best of friends, at some point you might need to accept that they just don't like each other. Lesley recalls feeling 'gob smacked' by this realization:

The psychologist said to me, 'They don't really like each other, do they, and it's fine for them not to'. My first thought was, 'Whatever do you mean? How can you say it's alright not to like each other?' But once I had thought about it, it made sense. Just the fact of knowing that and being able to deal with it has made it so much easier for me.'

Lesley immediately stopped trying to put her sons together. 'The minute I stopped trying to make them get on, it was easier. Now I don't try to get them to do the same things. They go with different friends, and next year they're going to different schools. They need their own identity and separate space,' she reflects.

It's very normal for siblings not to like each other,' says psychotherapist Julie Lynn-Evans.

Often they don't until they grow older and they find common ground; but while they are younger they often don't choose the same friends or play together in playgrounds, they have separate lives. When my son and my daughter hated each other I accepted that. I wouldn't permit disrespect or trashing each other's rooms, but otherwise I would shrug it off. Now they really like each other. But you can't have a saccharine forced family. It's dishonest.

If your children don't get on, you might find it helps to minimize the conflict by giving them less time together. This can mean finding different things for them to do, such as separate outings or friends, separate time with parents or even different schools.

'My brother and I operated on different wavelengths,' says Alex of his stormy relationship with his brother, Tom. 'He was sporty, I was a swot. I was jealous of his sporting prowess. He was more confident in a group, I was a loner.' The brothers were frequently in conflict and their parents eventually separated them by sending them to different schools. 'We just couldn't be at the same school,' says Alex, 'but it helped foster our individual identities.'

Between the ages of six and eleven, the brothers also went on separate holidays with different family members, because they were too much of a handful together. 'Our in-laws refused to have them both together,' remembers their mother Trish, 'so each set of parents would take one child. That worked for everybody.'

'What's important,' says Julie Lynn-Evans 'is for children to simply accept that the other child does exist and is in their life, and they just need to get on with it. Then they can stop trying to annihilate each other. If one child is constantly rejecting another, you need to find ways of helping that child deal with it.'

While you might have done everything you can to build a bond between your children, you might simply have to accept the way they feel. I have several friends who no longer speak to their siblings. In some families it just doesn't work.

'She never liked me – ever,' says Jacquie of her younger sister.

> *She always thought I was my mother's favourite and no one could convince her otherwise. She used to beat our brother up at primary school and steal his lunch money. Neither of us speaks to her now. She really is dead to me. I have girlfriends who feel more like sisters to me than she ever was.*

Nothing lasts forever

Even if your children don't get on now, it's worth remembering that all is not lost because, if there's one thing that's true about raising kids, it's that nothing stays the same.

As children go through changes in their lives outside the house, as they change schools and make new friends, it can impact on their relationship, for better or worse. Lisa's two elder children, twelve-year-old Amy and ten-year-old Henry both got on really well until a year ago. 'Now they are total rivals,' says Lisa. 'This has developed over the past year. No matter what they do, or say, they cannot agree on anything much at all, and invariably, it ends up in shouting matches.'

'What parents need to bear in mind is that as relationships develop there is a lot of continuity and a lot of change,' says psychologist Professor Judy Dunn.

Parents need endless patience and good humour and to retain that sense that this phase will pass. Our long-term studies showed us how siblings go through different transitions, how they get on at one point and not at another. I remember one family I interviewed, the siblings were very sweet when they were little; then I interviewed them again at ten and six and the older sister gave a wonderful account of the things they did together; yet when we asked the little brother what he liked about her, he said nothing!

Brothers Alex and Tom who had fought so vigorously and been so different that they were sent to different schools eventually ended up at the same school in the sixth form. Suddenly Alex shifted from being Tom's rival to being his defender. 'Someone bullied him and I ended up in huge trouble for hanging the bully out of a window,' recalls Alex. This was a turning-point for Tom:

[Alex] was very protective, and I was surprised by his loyalty and affection. It made me look at him in a different light. Once we realized that we occupied different parts of the universe, we began to get on. Now I adore the things that make him who he is; the differences in him are qualities I admire.

177

Postscript

Last night as the house settled into darkness I realized that it was completely quiet. I went looking for the children and heard murmuring from my daughter's room. Peeping round the door was a blissfully peaceful scene: three children in pyjamas, my elder son and daughter with heads bent over sticker books, quietly discussing which ones to swap with each other; my younger son curled up on the bed half listening to them and half looking at a book. I know you're meant to notice and praise them when they're getting along well, but I didn't want to interrupt and quietly crept away.

And so I've come to see while I've been writing this book that my children actually don't fight as much as I thought they did. By observing them over the past few months I've noticed far more of the jokes they share, the games they play and the many acts of cooperation and kindness that they show to each other, and at times how united they are against me. 'Please don't be cross with him Mum,' my youngest son said to me in the car this morning as I berated his elder brother for forgetting his bag. They know how to look out for each other and comfort each other every bit as much as they know how to push each other's buttons and inflict pain. They still fight, and still bicker incessantly at breakfast, but I've become far fiercer in putting a stop to it. As for the rest of it, well that's down to them. I hope they stay friends.

References and Resources

I referenced material from the following books and papers.

General books

Cousins, Lucy, *Za-Za's Baby Brother* (Walker Books Ltd., 2003)

Dunn, Judy and Kendrick, Carol, *Siblings: Love, Envy and Understanding* (Grant McIntyre, 1982)

Dunn, Judy and Plomin, Robert, *Separate Lives: Why Siblings Are So Different* (Basic Books, 1990)

Goldenthal, Peter, *Beyond Sibling Rivalry* (Owl Books, 1999)

Parker, Jan and Stimpson, Jan, *Sibling Rivalry, Sibling Love* (Hodder and Stoughton, 1992)

Plomin, R, DeFries, JC and Fulker, DW, *Nature and Nurture During Infancy and Early Childhood* (Cambridge University Press, 1988)

Wagner, Hilory, *And Baby Makes Four* (Avon Books, 1998)

Faber, Adele and Mazlish, Elaine, *Siblings Without Rivalry* (WW Norton and Co., 1987)

Journals and periodicals

Koch, HL, 'The relation of certain formal attributes of siblings to attitudes held towards each other and towards their parents', *Monographs of the Society for Research in Child Development* 25:4, 1960

Kramer, L and Gottman, JM, 'Becoming a sibling "with a little help from my friends"', *Developmental Psychology* 28:4:685–99

Perozynski, L and Kramer, L, 'Parental beliefs about managing sibling conflict', *Developmental Psychology* 5:32

Stocker, C, Dunn, J and Plomin, R, 'Sibling relationships: links with child temperament, maternal behaviour and family structure', *Child Development* 60:715–27, 1989

Web resources
The following websites provide general parenting advice and feedback, including tips on siblings.

www.bbc.co.uk/parenting
www.mumsnet.com
www.parentlineplus.org.uk
www.raisingkids.co.uk